Eco-Games:

Outdoor Science Simulations For Life and Earth Systems

By Jennifer Baron

Eco-Games: Outdoor Science Simuations for Life and Earth Science

ISBN: 978-1-7380722-2-4

*For Environmental and
Outdoor Educators,
who work to make our world
a better place
one step at a time.*

Table of Contents

Introduction

Children of all ages love games. Educators can turn this natural affinity to their advantage by using games as an instructional strategy. In fact, teachers have been doing so for years most commonly in Physical Education. In this book, educators will learn games that cover ecological concepts and environmental topics. I wrote this book to coincide with *The Ontario Curriculum*; particularly the *Life and Earth Systems* Strands in the *Science Curriculum, Grades 1-8*. Educators may wish to change the names of species in the games to match their local habitats; however, the concepts are universally applicable and important. As well, the format can be applied to most schoolyard settings. Ideally, children will have the opportunity to play these games outside. The schoolyard does not have to be naturalized or be adjacent to a naturalized space, although it is excellent if it is. In a pinch, the games can be played in a wide-open indoor space, such as a school gymnasium. So read on, be safe and have fun.

How to use this book

All of the games follow the same format. Learn the format and apply it to each game. Read "In a Nutshell" Game Format instructions first to get the general idea of the games. For more detailed instructions, refer to "The Nitty-Gritty" Details to get a complete set of instructions. As well, write-ups for each game include the following:

- Ecological Explanation
- Specific Instructions
- Extension activities and assessment suggestions
- Literacy Links
- Web Links

At the end of this book, there is a section on applying schoolyard mapping and orienteering skills to the games.

I usually start the games by reading aloud one of the excellent picture books that are sited in the Literacy Links section of the specific game instructions. From there, I explain the ecology, or environmental science behind the game. I include a discussion on the factors that are limiting the health of life and earth systems, such as pollution and habitat destruction. Then I go on to explain the game instructions. The indoor portion of the explanation usually takes roughly twenty minutes to half an hour.

After going over the map and boundaries, I take the class outside to play the game. Following the exact instructions in the "Nitty-Gritty" details, the outside portion takes roughly forty minutes.

Try one or more of the Extension Activities and Assessment Suggestions. The games really introduce these activities well, so that students have the basic vocabulary to express ideas in the follow-up tasks. Also, listed web sites contain many more relevant resources and ideas.

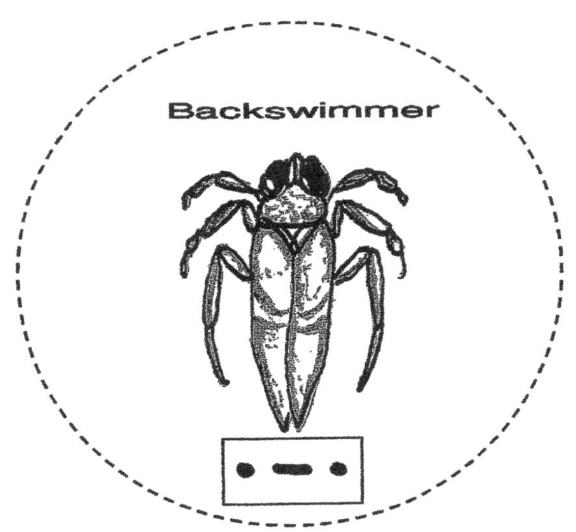

Here is an example of a game sign.

The Wetland Game		Name:	Points:
Backswimmer	Leech	Dragonfly Larva	Crayfish
Whirligig Beetle	Low Oxygen	Dip-net	Giant Water Bug
Stonefly Nymph	Acid Rain	Invertebrate Biologist	Freshwater Shrimp
Predacious Diving Beetle	Aquatic Worm	Mosquito Larva	Water Strider

Above is an example of a game card. Students have to find the game signs hidden in the playing area. When they find a game sign, they copy the Morse code symbol from the game sign into the matching box on the game card. They just got two points and the object of each game is to get as many points as possible. Part way through the game, the teacher chooses two students to be limiting factors, in the case above that would be Low Oxygen and Acid Rain. Resume the game. Students have to find the remaining game signs and stay away from the limiting factors, who can tag the rest of the students. Each time the limiting factor tags a student, they take away one Popsicle stick, worth one point, and mark the card in their role box with a minus one. If students go out of bounds in the game, the boundary patroller puts a minus one on the game card in the box for boundary patrol, in the game above that would be Dip-net. Teachers have the role of trouble-shooter in the game, in this case Invertebrate Biologist. The teacher can put in positive or negative marks, depending on the terms they set out with the class during the instructions.

When the game is over, students add up their points on their card. Then they use the Morse Code chart to de-code their symbols. They must unscramble the letters to attain the secret environmental message. See what a completed card might look like below.

Although these game instructions may sound a little tricky at first, kids love the scavenger hunt; physical activity; tag element and decoding the secret message. The high level of engagement that you will observe in students will make the initial set-up of these games worthwhile!

The Wetland Game		Name: Jane Smith	Points: 24
Backswimmer L	**Leech** S	**Dragonfly Larva** E	**Crayfish** W
Whirligig Beetle D	**Low Oxygen** −1	**Dip-net**	**Giant Water Bug** A
Stonefly Nymph S	**Acid Rain**	**Invertebrate Biologist** +1	**Freshwater Shrimp** E
Predacious Diving Beetle V	**Aquatic Worm** A	**Mosquito Larva** N	**Water Strider** T

Secret environmental message: SAVE WETLANDS

CRACK THE CODE

Each game has a secret environmental message that the players have to discover.

No.	The Game	Secret environmental message
1	Bird	HELP OUR BIRDS
2	Water Form	SAVE OUR WATER
3	Fish	CONSERVE FISH
4	Reptiles and Amphibians	REPTILES ROCK; SAVE THE FROGS; WHO IS A LIZARD
5	Plant	PLANT FLOWERS
6	Tree	PREVENT FIRES
7	Insect	BAN PESTICIDE
8	Rock Cycle	COLLECT ROCKS
9	Endangered Species	CARE TO CHANGE
10	Energy	CONSERVE HEAT
11	Oceans	SAVE OUR SEAS!
12	Wetland Ecosystems	SAVE WETLANDS
13	Carbon Cycle	CONSERVE FUEL
14	Water Systems	CLEAN UP WATER
15	Planet Earth	SAVE OUR WORLD; LOVE THE EARTH; WE ALL CONNECT.

Each of the above messages contains twelve letters. The English letters correspond to the symbols in the Morse code alphabet below.

Educators must write on each game sign for that particular game the Morse code symbol for one English letter from the secret message above. The game card sign templates do not have the Morse code symbols on them on purpose. This is so that educators may change the secret message to their own, or scramble the symbols differently each time they play the game.

Players must record the Morse code symbol in the box on the game card that matches the word and picture on the game sign. Once players have found all 12 game signs and recorded the Morse code symbols on the game card, then they need to crack the code. They do this by looking at the Morse code chart and decoding the symbols to match the letters of the English alphabet. Once they have all twelve letters, they must unscramble them to discover the secret environmental message.

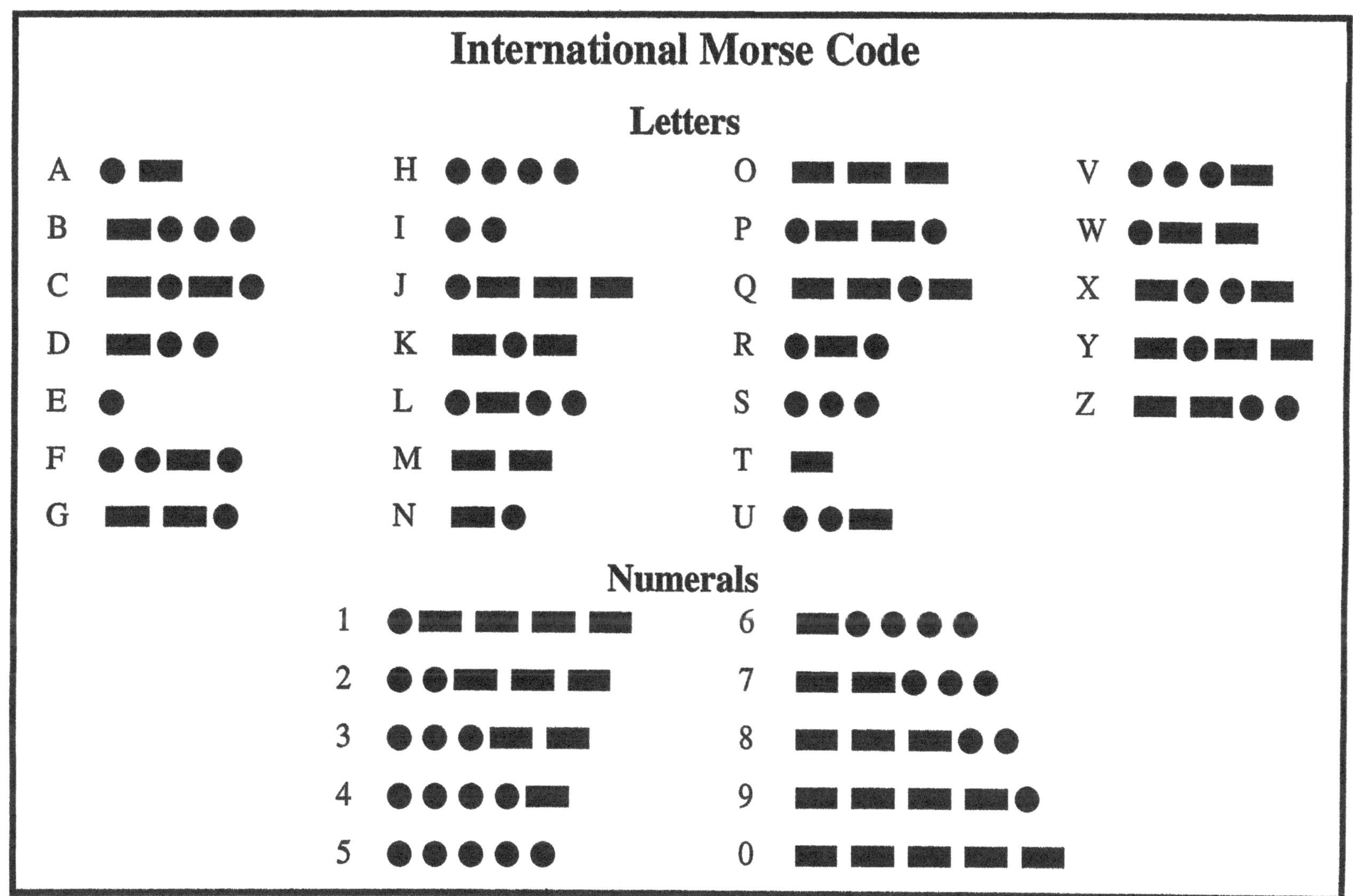

International Morse Code
Letters
A ●■
B ■●●●
C ■●■●
D ■●●
E ●
F ●●■●
G ■■●
H ●●●●
I ●●
J ●■■■
K ■●■
L ●■●●
M ■■
N ■●
O ■■■
P ●■■●
Q ■■●■
R ●■●
S ●●●
T ■
U ●●■
V ●●●■
W ●■■
X ■●●■
Y ■●■■
Z ■■●●
Numerals
1 ●■■■■
2 ●●■■■
3 ●●●■■
4 ●●●●■
5 ●●●●●
6 ■●●●●
7 ■■●●●
8 ■■■●●
9 ■■■■●
0 ■■■■■

"The Nitty-Gritty" Instructional Details

Materials
- Class set of game cards.
- 12 game signs.
- 2 popsicle sticks per student.
- 2 brightly coloured sports vests.
- Class set of writing utensils (pencils in good weather/permanent markers in inclement weather).
- Whistle.

Safety considerations:
- Carry a first aid kit that includes plastic gloves for the first aid provider.
- Have a communications system on hand, whether that be a walkie-talkie to speak with someone in your facility that has phone access, or carry a cell phone.
- Go over the boundaries and the playing area to make sure it's safe before you play the game.

Preparation

Game cards:
- Photocopy class set (2 fit on one 8 ½ x 11" paper).
- Laminate if playing in inclement weather.

Signs:
- Photocopy set of 12 (enlarge if needed or wanted).
- Cut out.
- Hide within boundaries of game on trees, bushes, posts or other structures, placing them at students' eye level so that when they find the placard they will be able to see clearly the words and symbols on them.

Boundaries:
- Choose a playing area large enough for the whole class to run around and with places for hiding 12 signs.
- Use obvious pre-existing boundaries such as fences and sidewalks or mark boundaries with brightly coloured pylons or flagging tape.
- Mark a site in the middle of the playing area as home base by using a pre-existing landmark such as a mound, post or large rock, or create one by placing a hoola-hoop on the ground.

The Lesson

Ecological Explanation:
- Explain the background information that that the students need to know to play the game.

- Explain the background information that that the students need to know to play the game.
- Each game has Literacy Links. Read-alouds help to introduce the concepts the students need to have prior to the game.

General Game Instructions

- Clearly go over the game boundaries and the whistle signal for returning to home base.
- Start the game at home base.
- The first object of the game is for students to find as many of the elements on the 12 hidden signs throughout the playing area as possible.
- When students find a sign, they match the element on the sign to the one on their game card, then they write the Morse Code symbol in that element's box on the game card. See below.

Name:		Points:	
Ex. Snow ● ▬ ●	Element	Element	Element
Element	Limiting Factor	Boundary Patrol	Element
Element	Limiting Factor	Conservation Officer	Element
Element	Element	Element	Element

Format of Game Card   Format of sign

- Each correctly completed box is worth 2 points.
- Before students have had a chance to find all 12 signs, blow the whistle to signal to students to come back to home base.
- Count to make sure all students have returned.
- Choose two students to be limiting factors. These students don brightly coloured sports vests for easy identification.
- Give all the rest of the students two popsicle sticks. Each popsicle stick is worth one point.
- Now the game begins again and there are two objects. Object number one is for students to find the rest of the element signs. Object number two is for students to stay away from the limiting factors, who can tag them.
- When a limiting factor tags a student, he or she takes away one of the student's popsicle sticks. This means the tagged student loses one point. They also draw a circle with an X through it on the box that corresponds to their limiting factor. This means the student who got tagged loses another point.
- Tag fairness rules include no tag backs: the limiting factor must tag another student in between tagging the same student twice. Students can only get tagged a maximum of two times, as that is how many popsicle sticks they have. Also, it's a one-hand tag, not a two-hand tackle: it's not football! Finally, there are no time

outs. Students are not on time out while they are writing down an element from a sign, as that would be unrealistic to the nature of the limiting factors in real life. Students may go to home base before the game ends only if they are hurt; otherwise, it's not a time out haven.

- Adult volunteers; students who may be unable to actively participate in the game that day; other assistants may be boundary patrol. Students lose one point if they go out of bounds. Boundary patrollers mark a minus one (-1) on the game card box designated for that purpose in the game.
- The teacher has the role of conservation officer, or a specific title such as that depending on the game. The Conservation Officer work for or against the students, depending on their behaviour. The educator's role is really a trouble-shooting, management one. If students are doing everything right in the game and they are able to give the Conservation Officer a fact that they learned from the indoor lesson on the topic of the game, then the teacher can put a positive number of points in the Conservation Officer box. Limit it to +1 per fact though, or it skews the points at the end of the game. Alternatively, if students are misbehaving, such as pushing in line to see the signs or copying off of each other's cards, then the teacher can put negative points in the Conservation Officer box.
- At the end of the game, blow the whistle to signal students to return to home base.
- Tally up the points. Give two points for every box with the correct symbol that matches the element. Add or subtract points based upon the format above.
- Get limiting factors to add up the number of Popsicle sticks they have.
- De-brief according to the specific explanation per each game.
- Once the students have their points recorded on their game card, have them decode and unscramble the secret message. It may be necessary to do this step inside where a decoding chart can be put on an overhead and students can write on a flat surface.
- Follow the extensions per each game.
- Mapping and orienteering skills can be added to each game. For further instructions on this, go to the last section of the book.

Modifications

There are a number of modifications one can add to make the games more difficult. Very simply, these include:

- Adding mapping and orienteering skills. See the last section of the book for more detailed instructions on how to do this.
- Use a larger playing area.
- Hide the games signs in spots that are more difficult for students to find, such as far below or just above eye level, but not beyond reach.
- Follow the games by trying some of the Extension Activities and Assessment Suggestions. Students will gain a deeper understanding of the ecological concepts and environmental issues introduced in the games.
- Photocopy the game signs on to card stock or heavy paper that is the same colour as the background where you will hide them. For example, use light brown for tree trunks, or white when there is a lot of snow on the ground.

<u>The Bird Game Instructions</u>

Ecological Explanation

Children are fascinated with birds in large part due to their power of flight. Children delight in finding a feather, feeding birds and watching them fly up high in the sky. Older students may wish to identify birds not only by their appearance, but also by their song.

In the bird game, children will have the opportunity to identify many birds by their appearance. They will also learn of three of the problems that birds face and some of the solutions that they can do to help them.

To start, like all species, birds are dependent on their habitat for survival. The importance of habitat is slightly made more complex when one considers that birds migrate, and are thus dependent on more than one habitat range. For example, close to 200 species of birds, equaling over 1 billion birds in total, fly to Canada's boreal forest in the spring to feed on the explosion of insect life. In the fall, these same birds migrate to the southern United States, Mexico and the Caribbean. Therefore, they depend on the integrity of the habitat in both of their habitats. Deforestation and wetland destruction are serious problems that effect bird's populations.

Secondly, in urban areas, birds are often attracted to the lights that shine in the night from a tall skyscraper, or the reflection of the sky in a window. The birds collide with the building and fall to the ground. Many children have had the experience of trying to nurse a bird back to health after it has hit the window.

Finally, domestic cats love to eat birds. Many a comic has dwelt on this all too familiar concept. However, to the beautiful songbirds that share our human and domestic animal spaces, this is a deadly serious matter.

Specific Instructions

In The Bird Game, students have to run around the playing area searching for the twelve game signs, which each have a different bird picture and name on them. When they find a game sign, they record the Morse code symbol in the box on the game card that matches the bird picture and name on the game sign. The boundary patrollers take on the role of house cat.

Part way through the game, blow the whistle and have students come back to home base. The educator chooses two students to be the limiting factors of habitat loss and fatal light attraction. The remaining students get two Popsicle sticks, which each represent a single bird. Begin the game again and follow the instructions in the Game Format chapter.

Blow the whistle at the end of the game to signal all students to return to home base. Tally up the points. The points on a game card represent the number of birds that player saved. The Limiting Factors' Popsicle sticks represent the number of birds that succumbed to habitat loss and fatal light attraction.

Give the students the Morse code alphabet. Students must decode the Morse code alphabet into English letters and then unscramble the letters to find the secret environmental message: SAVE THE BIRDS.

Extension Activities and Assessment Suggestions

Students could:
1) Research the migratory patterns and habitat ranges of a specific bird and present their findings in an interesting way;
2) Research the feeding and nesting needs of birds and create bird feeders and nesting boxes;
3) Create a pamphlet raising the awareness of bird's attraction to light at night. They could lobby companies to turn out the lights at night: this also conserves energy;
4) Create silhouettes of hawks and tape them to the inside of picture windows, thereby detracting from a bird's tendency to fly into the window;
5) Research the topic of house cats that prey on songbirds and debate the many choices people have to remedy this problem.

Literature Links

Arnosky, Jim. <u>Crinkleroot's 25 birds every child should know.</u> New York: Bradberry Press, 1993.

Boring, Mel. <u>Birds, Nests and Eggs.</u> Chanhassen, MN: NorthWord Press, 1996.

Glew, Frank. <u>Chickadee Chatter.</u>

Hickman, Pamela & Federation of Ontario Naturalis. <u>Bird Wise.</u> Toronto: Kids Can Press, 1988.

Sill, Cathryn P., <u>About Birds.</u> Atlanta, GA: Peachtree Publishers, 1991.

Web Links

www.flap.org for information on fatal light awareness and sky reflection in windows.

www.borealbirds.org for conservation of boreal forest songbird habitat.

www.birdfeeding.org for solutions on domestic cats preying on songbirds.

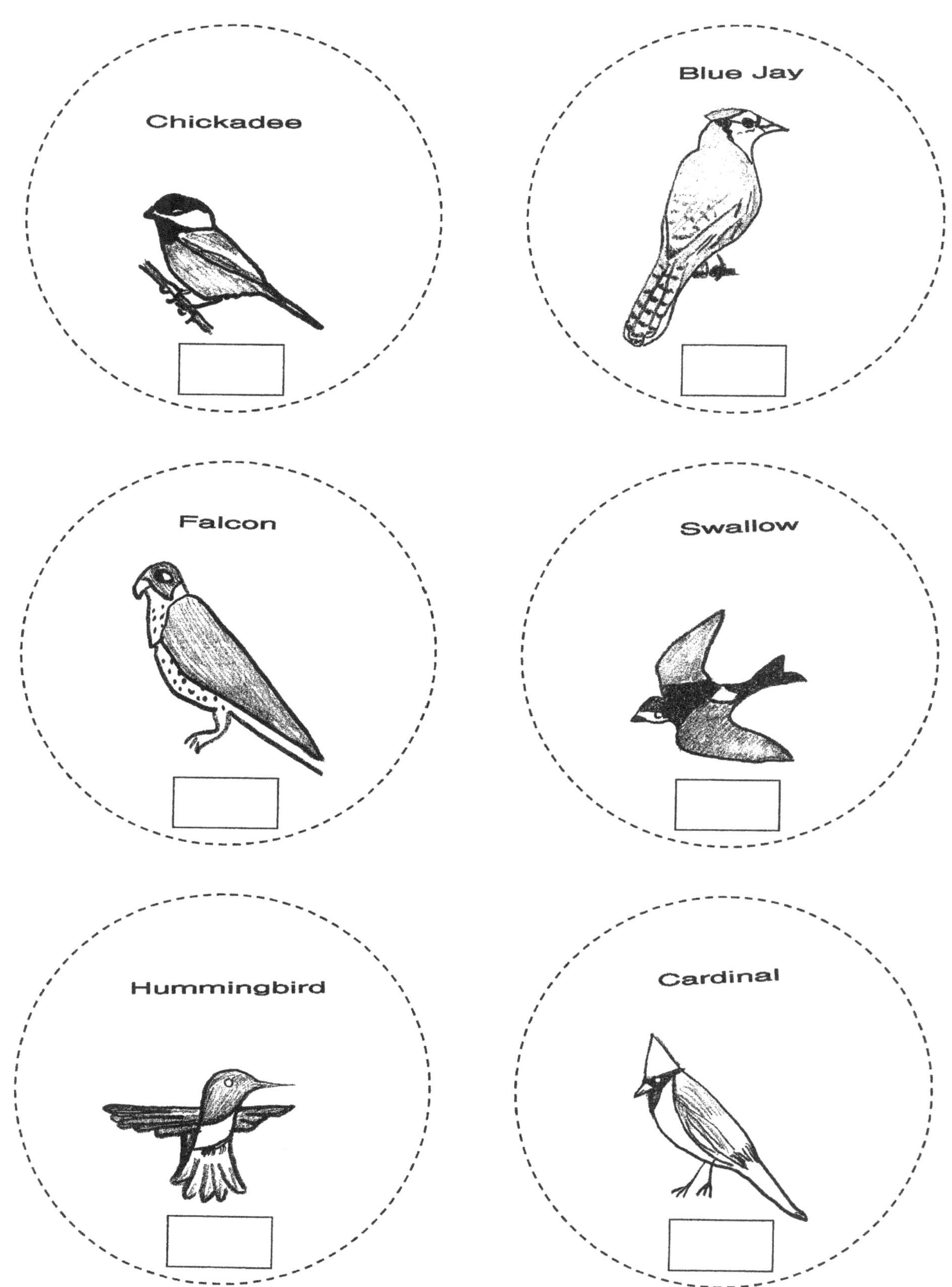
Chickadee
Blue Jay
Falcon
Swallow
Hummingbird
Cardinal

Spotted Owl
Canada Goose
Common Loon
Nuthatch
Goldfinch
Trumpeter Swan

The Bird Game		Name:	Points:
Chickadee	Bluejay	Canada Goose	Swallow
Hummingbird	Fatal Light Attraction	House cat	Cardinal
Spotted Owl	Habitat Loss	Ornithologist	Falcon
Common Loon	Goldfinch	Nuthatch	Trumpeter Swan

The Bird Game		Name:	Points:
Chickadee	Bluejay	Canada Goose	Swallow
Hummingbird	Fatal Light Attraction	House cat	Cardinal
Spotted Owl	Habitat Loss	Ornithologist	Falcon
Common Loon	Goldfinch	Nuthatch	Trumpeter Swan

<u>The Fish Game</u>

Ecological Explanation

North America contains a bounty of millions of freshwater lakes, including the largest freshwater system on Earth, the Great Lakes. A wide diversity of freshwater fish live in these lakes. They are an integral part of the freshwater ecosystem in which they live. Fish require a clan, stable environment in which to spawn, grow and migrate. Every life-stage from egg to adult has special needs for survival. Fish become vulnerable when their fragile habitat is disrupted by the activities of people, such as obstructions from dams, roadway culverts, water extraction, shoreline destruction and improper disposal of trash.

For thousands of years, people of the First Nations of North America have caught the fish that live in those lakes. Avid fisherman continue to catch and release or consume great quantities of fish every year, making fishing a very important part of the North American economy. However, over-fishing is the single greatest ecological problem in relation to fish today. Conservation of fish to ensure a viable number for the survival of the species is essential.

The environmental problems that occur in lakes effect their inhabitants, namely the fish. For example, fertilizers and pesticides that people use on their gardens and fields enter the watershed and end up in lakes.

Large amounts of nitrogen and phosphorous cause algae to grow in vast amounts in the lakes. The algae dies causing microorganisms and bacteria to grow which use oxygen. This lowers the oxygen level in the lake, and then fish species, such as Lake Trout, which need a high level of dissolved oxygen cannot survive.

Many human made chemicals, such as polychlorinated biphenyls (PCBs), pesticides and insecticides, such as Mirex, Toxaphene and other chlorinated organic compounds, have entered freshwater lakes in the last fifty years. They bioaccumulate in the fatty tissue of fish. As a result, people must be aware of the recommended consumption restrictions for health reasons prior to eating freshwater fish.

Specific Instructions

In the Fish Game, students must run around the playing area and search for twelve game signs, each with a picture and name of a fish. When they find a game sign, they write the Morse code symbol in the box on the game card that matches the game sign. The boundary patrollers take on the role of dry land. The educator troubleshoots in the game as the Conservation Officer.

Part way through the game, blow the whistle and have students come back to home base. The educator chooses two students to be the limiting factors of phosphorous loading and contaminants. The remaining students get two Popsicle sticks, which each represent a single fish. Begin the game again and follow the instructions in the Game Format chapter.

Blow the whistle at the end of the game to signal all students to return to home base. Tally up the points. The points on a game card represent the numbers of fish that player saved. The Limiting Factors' Popsicle sticks represent the number of fish that succumbed to phosphorous loading and contaminants. Give the students the Morse code alphabet. Students must decode the Morse code alphabet into English letters and then unscramble the letters to find the secret environmental message: CONSERVE FISH.

Extension and Assessment Suggestions
Students could:
1) Research the reasons why there are consumption restrictions on freshwater fish and present their findings to the class;
2) Represent fish and freshwater ecosystems in an artistic display, such as a mural, diorama, drawing or painting. Watercolour over wax crayon works well for this;
3) Paint fish on local sewer covers to educate the community on the hazards of dumping oil, paint and other toxic chemicals down the drain or sewer;
4) Rehabilitate a shoreline, stream or river.

Literacy Links
Ministry of Natural Resources. <u>Fishways.</u> Ontario: Queen's Printer for Ontario, 1991.
Department of Fisheries and Oceans<u>. Fish Habitat Care.</u> New Brunswick: MacNab Print.
Ministry of the Environment. <u>Guide to Eating Ontario Sport Fish</u>. Ontario, Queen's Printer for Ontario: 2003.

Web Links
<u>www.ijc.org</u> for more on Great Lakes.
<u>www.mnr.gov.on.ca</u> for fishing information.
For more information on Contaminant Monitoring Program e-mail <u>sportfish@ene.gov.on.ca</u>

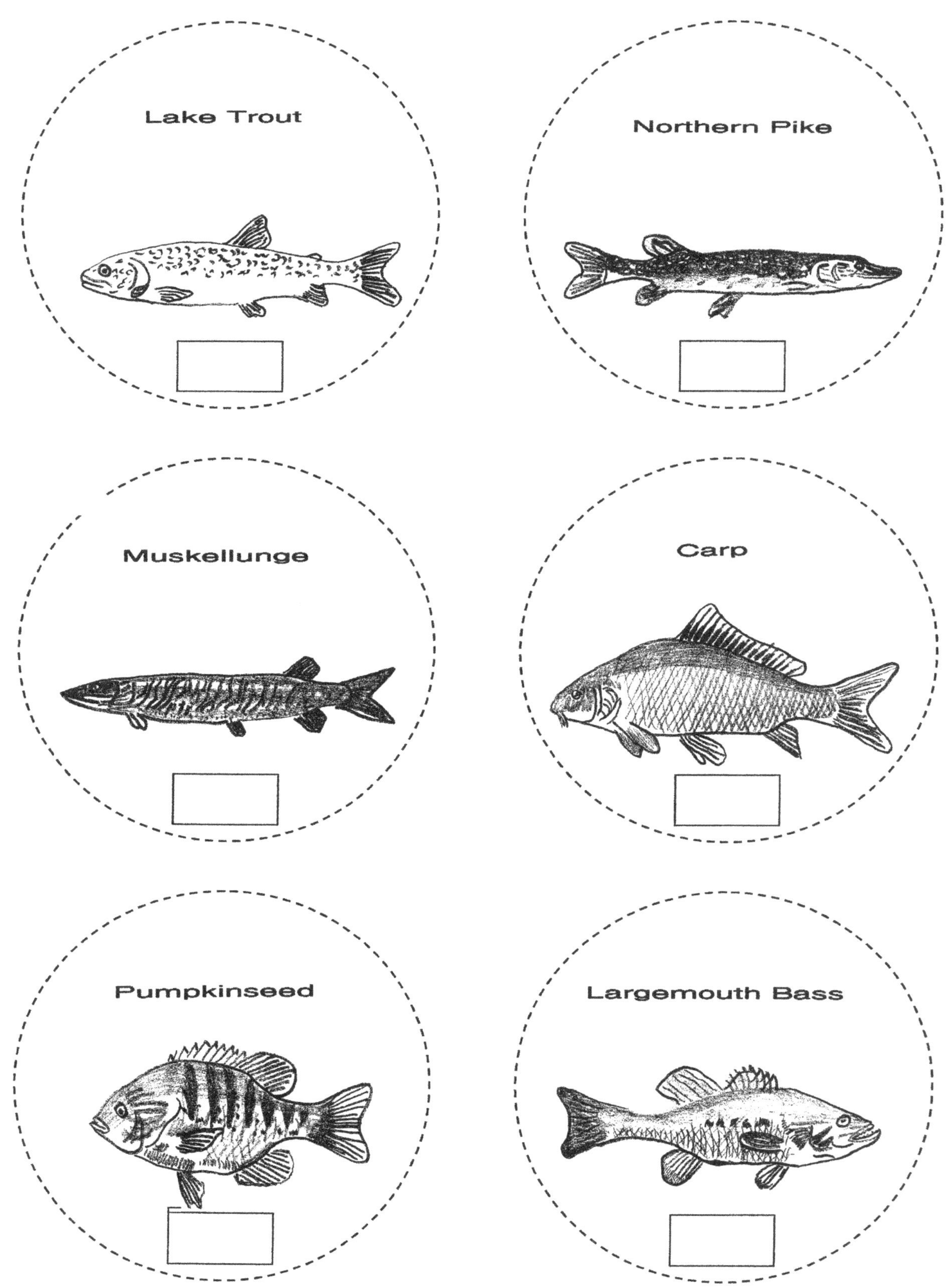

Lake Trout
Northern Pike
Muskellunge
Carp
Pumpkinseed
Largemouth Bass

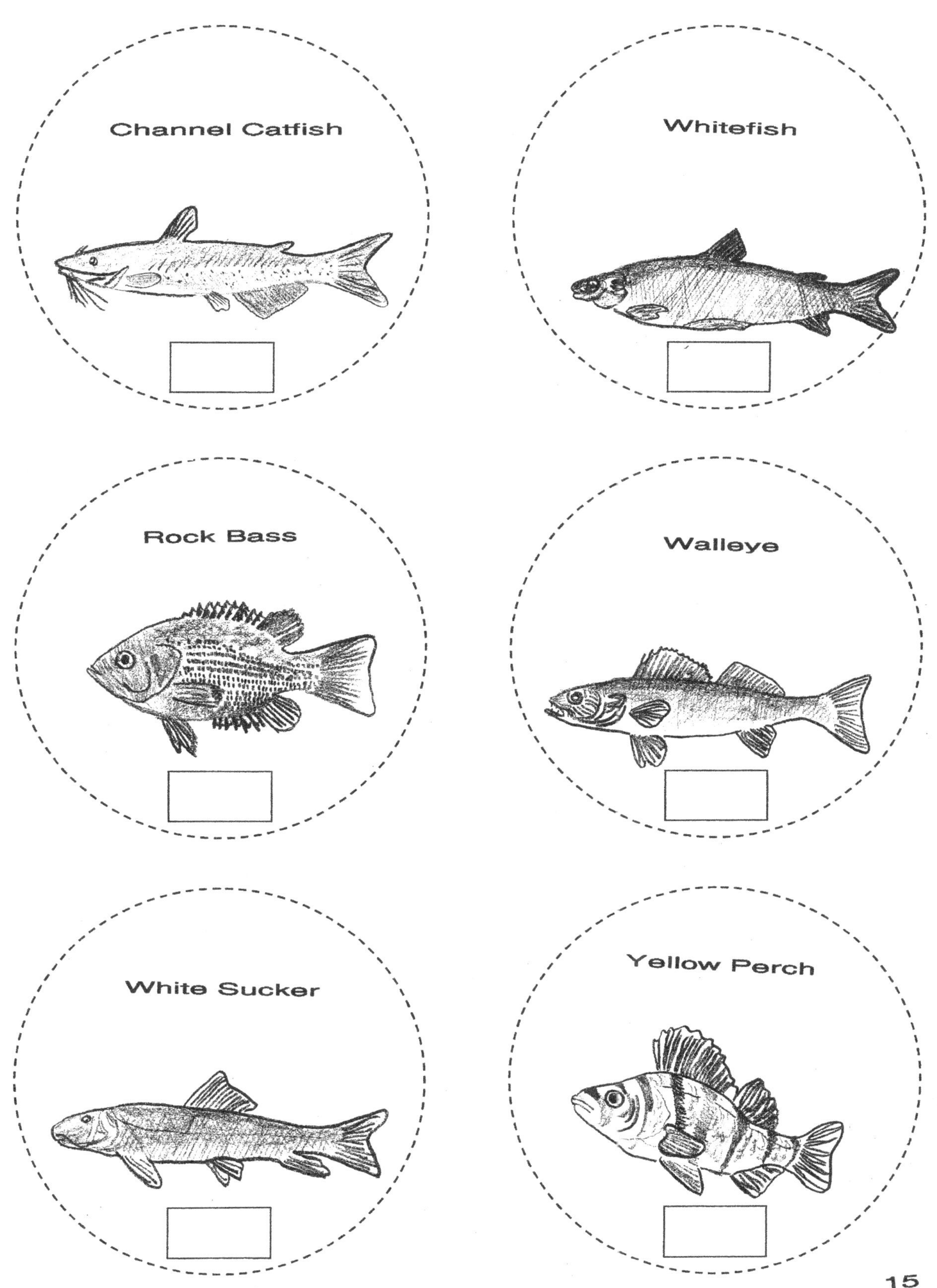

Channel Catfish
Whitefish
Rock Bass
Walleye
White Sucker
Yellow Perch

The Fish Game		Name:	Points:
Lake Trout	Northern Pike	Muskellunge	Carp
Pumpkinseed	Pollution	Boat	Largemouth Bass
Channel Catfish	Over-fishing	Conservation Officer	Lake Whitefish
Rock Bass	Walleye	White Sucker	Yellow Perch

The Fish Game		Name:	Points:
Lake Trout	Northern Pike	Muskellunge	Carp
Pumpkinseed	Pollution	Boat	Largemouth Bass
Channel Catfish	Over-fishing	Conservation Officer	Lake Whitefish
Rock Bass	Walleye	White Sucker	Yellow Perch

The Insect Game

Ecological Explanation

Children are more likely to be fascinated by creeping, crawling insects than adults as their fears and inhibitions have not developed as strongly. Certainly, a child who has been stung or has a bad allergy to a certain insect's bite may be more wary, but generally speaking, children are very curious about our six-legged friends.

Insects are the most abundant life form on earth and they can be readily found on any nature walk in the spring, summer and fall. Children love to roll over logs and rocks, dip-net and search in the tall grass to find insects.

Of course, most children are intrinsically aware that people consider some insects pests, such as mosquitoes and bees. However, children need to be made aware of the vital role insects play as food for so many other animals in the food web. Bats, for instance, depend on mosquitoes. Bees are essential for the pollination of flowers.

Children are also naturally attracted to some of the more colourful and beautiful insects, such as ladybugs and butterflies.

In this game, children will become aware of the damaging effects of spraying pesticide on lawns, gardens and crops. Pesticides are designed to poison the intended insect that is eating the plant the person wishes to see left unharmed. The effect of the pesticide does not end with the death of the intended insect. It gets into the food web, as animals feed on the insect with pesticide in it. The pesticide then accumulates in animals further along in the food web. The pesticide can have extremely harmful effects on these animals that end up with pesticide in them.

Like all other animals, insects are completely dependent upon their habitat for survival. Some insects have very specific habitats. For example, the Monarch butterfly comes to Canada to lay its eggs. The caterpillar feeds on the milkweed plant, then it pupates. Once the adult emerges from the chrysalis, it must migrate to the Oyamel forests of central Mexico to spend the winter. Millions of monarch butterflies depend on this very specific habitat in Mexico to spend the winter. If it was destroyed, then so would be the monarch butterfly.

Specific Instructions

In the Insect Game, students must run around the playing area and search for twelve game signs, each with a picture and name of an insect. When they find a game sign, they write the Morse code symbol in the box on the game card that matches the game sign. The boundary patrollers take on the role of net. The educator trouble shoots in the game as the entomologist.

Part way through the game, blow the whistle and have students come back to home base. The educator chooses two students to be the limiting factors of habitat loss and pesticide. The remaining students get two Popsicle sticks, which each represent a single insect. Begin the game again and follow the instructions in the Game Format chapter.

Blow the whistle at the end of the game to signal all students to return to home base. Tally up the points. The points on a game card represent the number of insects that player saved. The Limiting Factors' popsicles represents the number of insects that succumbed to habitat loss and pesticide.

Give the students the Morse code alphabet. Students must decode the Morse code alphabet into English letters and then unscramble the letters to find the secret environmental message: BAN PESTICIDE.

Extension Activities and Assessment Suggestions

1) Visit a wetland or field. Have students dip-net or dry net for insects. Take care not to harm the insects and their habitat during this investigation.
2) Visit a forest. Have students roll over logs and rocks to check for insects underneath. Be careful to return the rock or log exactly as it was as it provides essential shelter for the insect.
3) Students can research the roll one or more insects play in the food web and display this web on paper or in three-dimensional sculpture form.
4) Plant a butterfly garden. Assist an organization that protects butterfly habitat.

Literacy Links

Glew, Frank. <u>Butterfly Wishes.</u> Kitchener: Pmara Kutata Enterprises, 2003.

Godkin, Celia. <u>Ladybug Garden.</u> Markham: Fitzhenry & Whiteside, 1995.

Hickman, Pamela and The Federation of Ontario Naturalists. <u>Bug Wise.</u> Toronto: Kids Can Press, Ltd., 1990.

Web sites
www.butterflywebsite.com
www.caps.20m.com

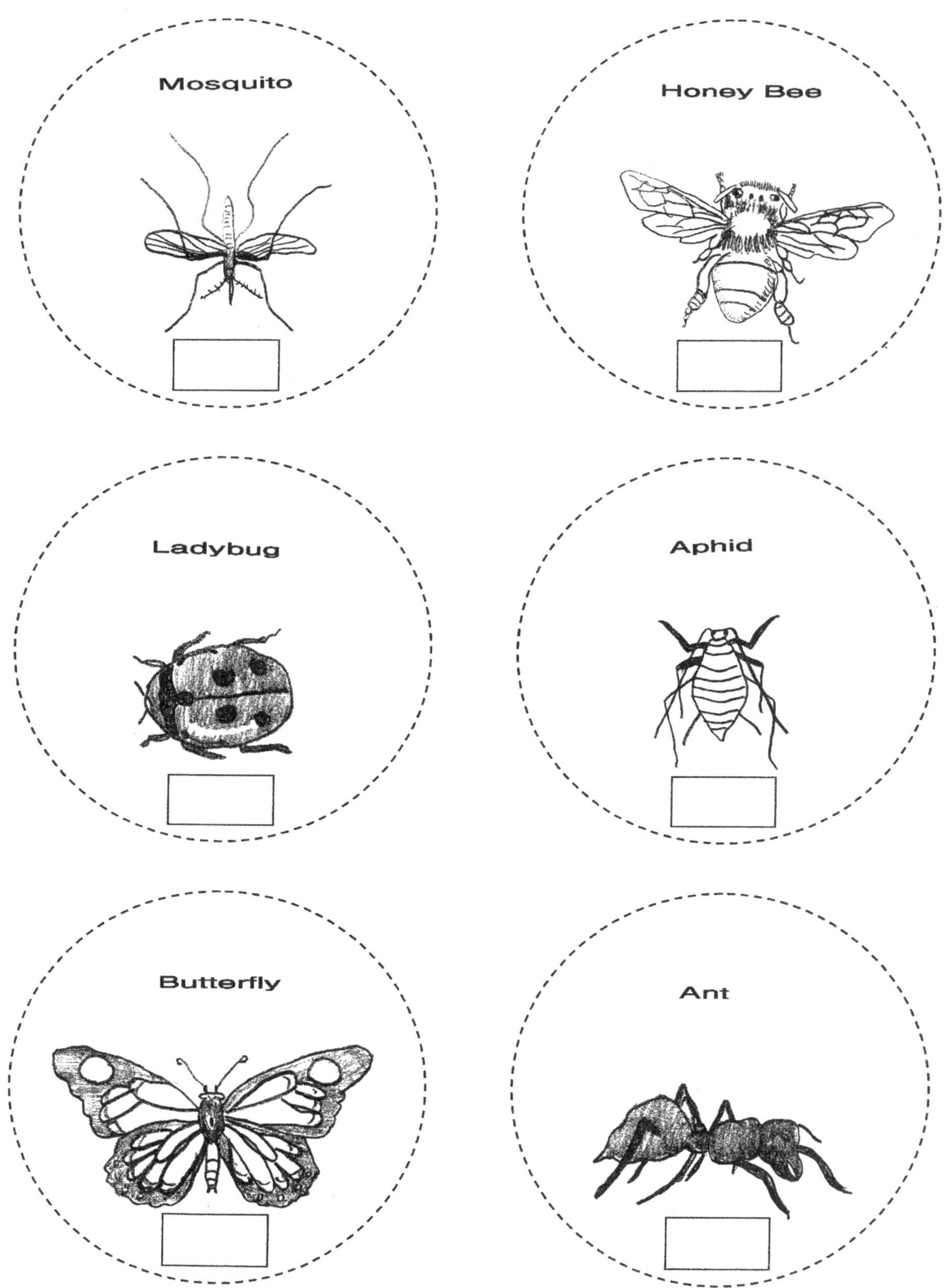

Mosquito
Honey Bee
Ladybug
Aphid
Butterfly
Ant

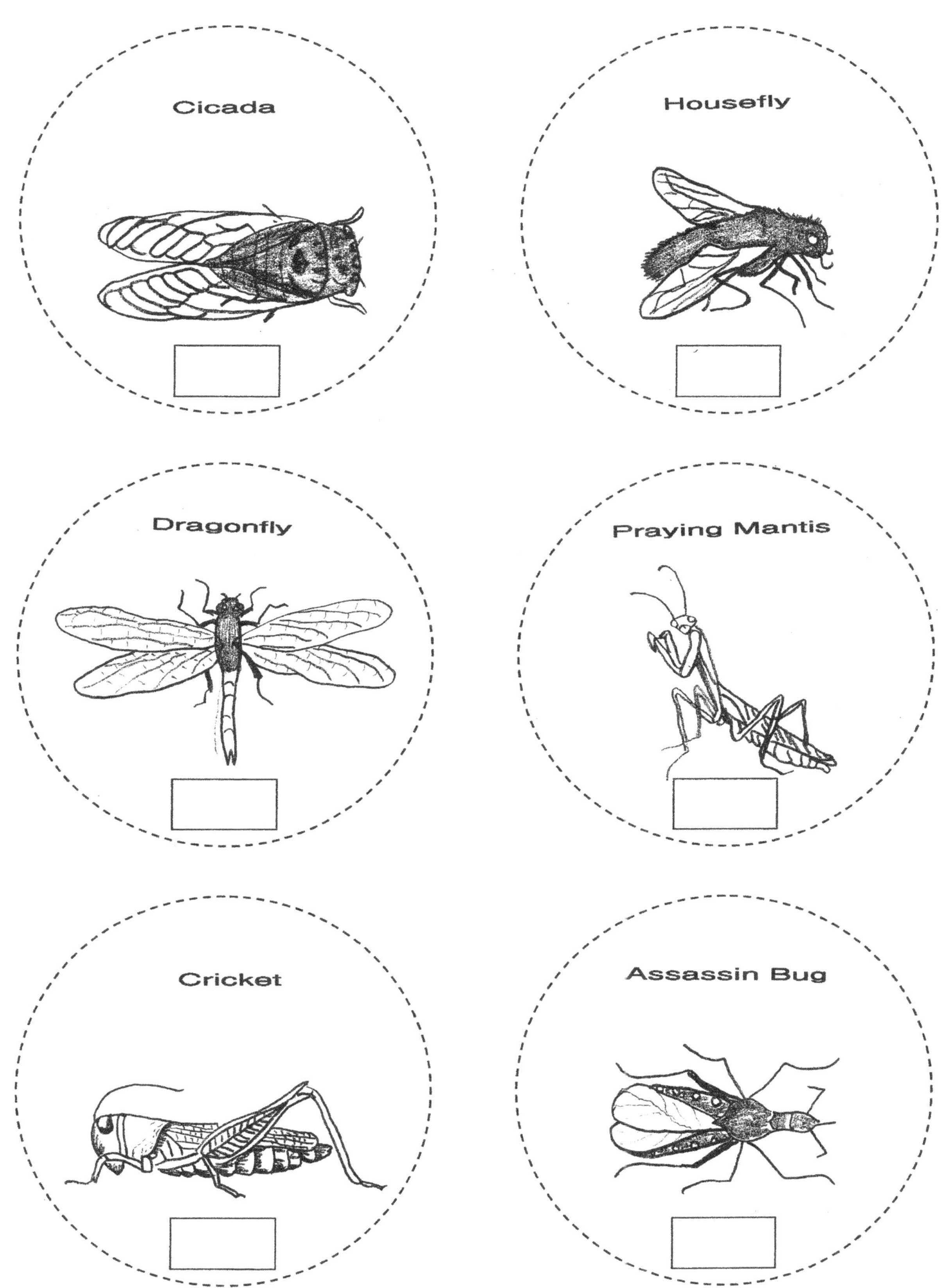

Cicada
Housefly
Dragonfly
Praying Mantis
Cricket
Assassin Bug

The Insect Game		Name:	Points:
Mosquito 	Honey Bee 	Ladybug 	Aphid 
Ant 	Pesticide	Net	Butterfly 
Cicada 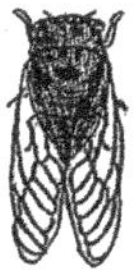	Habitat Loss	Entomologist	Housefly 
Dragonfly 	Praying Mantis 	Cricket 	Assassin Bug 

The Insect Game		Name:	Points:
Mosquito 	Honey Bee 	Ladybug 	Aphid 
Ant 	Pesticide	Net	Butterfly 
Cicada 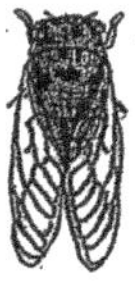	Habitat Loss	Entomologist	Housefly 
Dragonfly 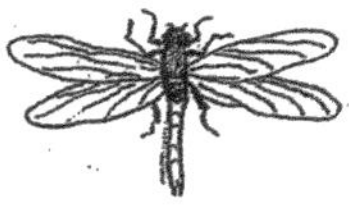	Praying Mantis 	Cricket 	Assassin Bug 

<u>The Amphibians and Reptiles Game</u>

Ecological Explanation

Amphibians have moist skin, while reptiles have dry skin. Both are cold-blooded; therefore, they hibernate in the winter. Children are much more likely to see these creatures on a warm, sunny day from late spring to early fall. Frogs and toads are the more common amphibians to children. Salamanders and newts are tailed amphibians. Children may be thrilled to find a salamander while they are exploring under rocks or logs in damp forests. Please read *"The Salamander Room"* prior to any exploring, and students will understand that keeping these animals in their habitats in the wild is the best place for them. The mudpuppy is the only amphibian with external gills. As such, they live completely in an aquatic environment. Any child who has ever caught a mudpuppy would surely agree that it was one of the most surprising catches of their lives, as the bright red gills and slippery nature of this bottom dweller is surely to startle the hardiest of naturalists.

During the warm months, children may spot a snake or turtle sunning itself on a rock or log in or near a wetland. Many children are not nearly as frightened of these animals as adults; in fact, I have found that they are exceedingly curious and want to learn more about them. During the breeding season, many amphibians and turtles seek the warmth of pavement, and the soft gravel of road shoulders to lay their eggs. Many of these animals lose their lives due to road mortality. I have had the sickening experience of observing a driver aim to run over what turned out to be an ancient snapping turtle. Now, I always carry a shovel, gloves, large container and a blanket to transport these beautiful creatures off the road and back to the wetland for safety.

All amphibians and many reptiles, such as turtles, depend on wetlands for breeding and hibernating. Wetlands support an incredible diversity of life, including reptiles and amphibians. Canada has about one quarter of the world's wetlands. Unfortunately, this vital habitat for plants and animals is disappearing around the world.

Another pitfall of reptiles in particular is illegal collection. There is one lizard in this game: the Five-lined Skink. Although children will be fascinated by this animal, and would love to see it in the wild, children should also appreciate that nature is where this beautiful animal belongs.

Specific Instructions

In The Amphibians and Reptiles Game, students have to run around the playing area searching for the twelve game signs, which each have a different amphibian or reptile on them. When they find a game sign, they record the Morse code symbol in the box on the game card that matches the animal on the game sign. The boundary patrollers take on the role of Illegal Collector. The teacher is the Conservation Officer.

Part way through the game, blow the whistle and have students come back to home base. The educator chooses two students to be the limiting factors of Habitat loss and Road Mortality. The remaining students get two Popsicle sticks, which each represent a single animal. Begin the game again and follow the instructions in the Game Format chapter.

Blow the whistle at the end of the game to signal all students to return to home base. Tally up the points. The points on a game card represent the number of amphibians and reptiles that player saved. The Limiting Factors' popsicles represents the number of animals that succumbed to habitat loss and road mortality.

Give the students the Morse code alphabet. Students must decode the Morse code alphabet into English letters and then unscramble the letters to find the secret environmental message: REPTILES ROCK, SAVE THE FROGS or WHO IS A LIZARD.

Extension Activities and Assessment Suggestions
1) Classify the animals on the game card into amphibians and reptiles.
2) Research which of these animals are considered Species at Risk, and learn what to do to help them.
3) Visit a wetland or roll over rock and logs in a moist forest to observe amphibians and reptiles. Discuss the importance of keeping them in their wild habitat.

Literatures Links

A Sample of Ontario's Amphibians and Reptiles. Poster. Ontario: Queen's Printer for Ontario, 1989.

Johnson, Bob. <u>Familiar Amphibians and Reptiles of Ontario.</u> Toronto: Natural Heritage/Natural History Inc., 1989.

Mazer, Anne. <u>The Salamander Room.</u> Canada: Random House of Canada. 1991.

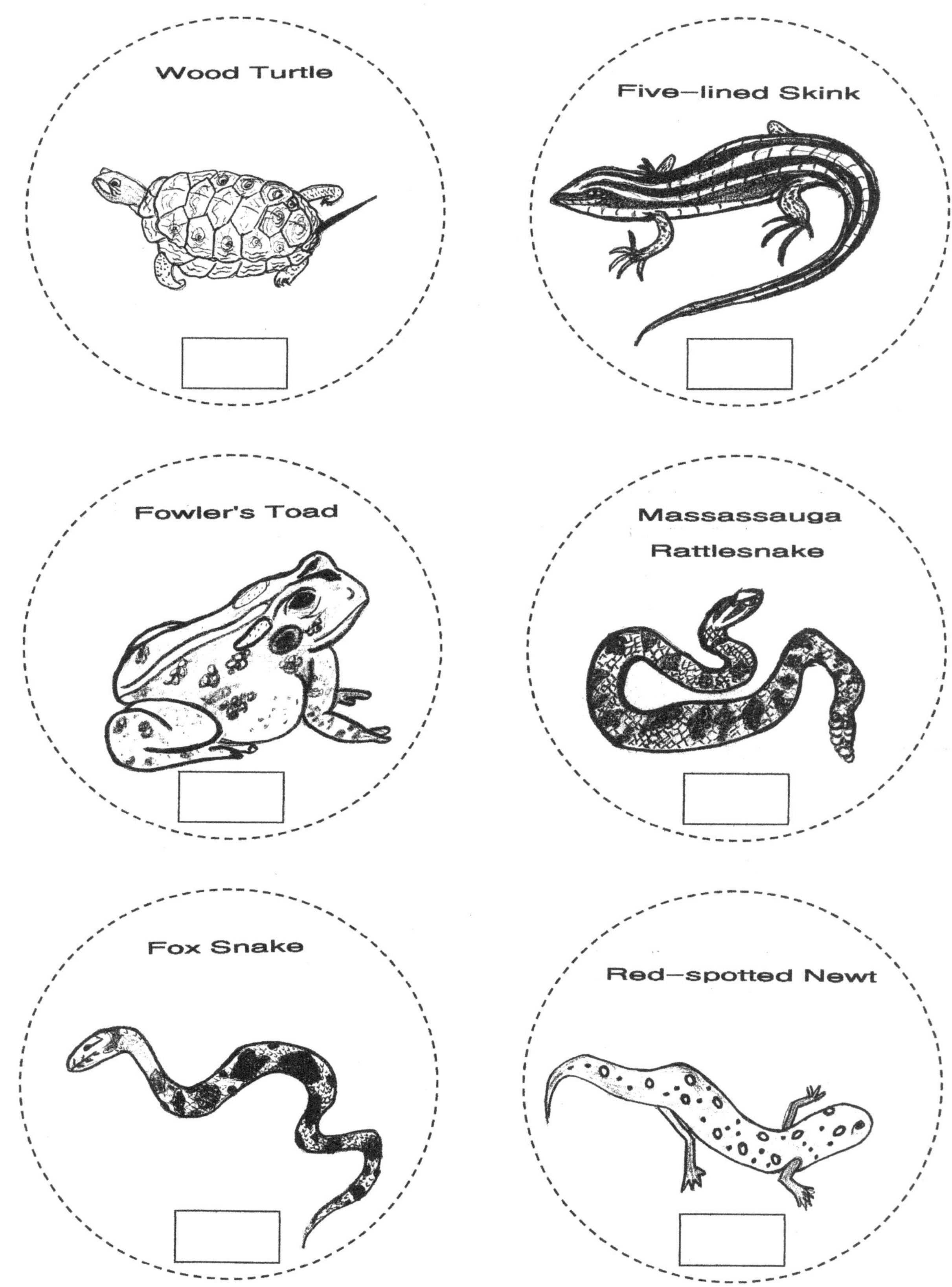

Wood Turtle
Five-lined Skink
Fowler's Toad
Massassauga
Rattlesnake
Fox Snake
Red-spotted Newt

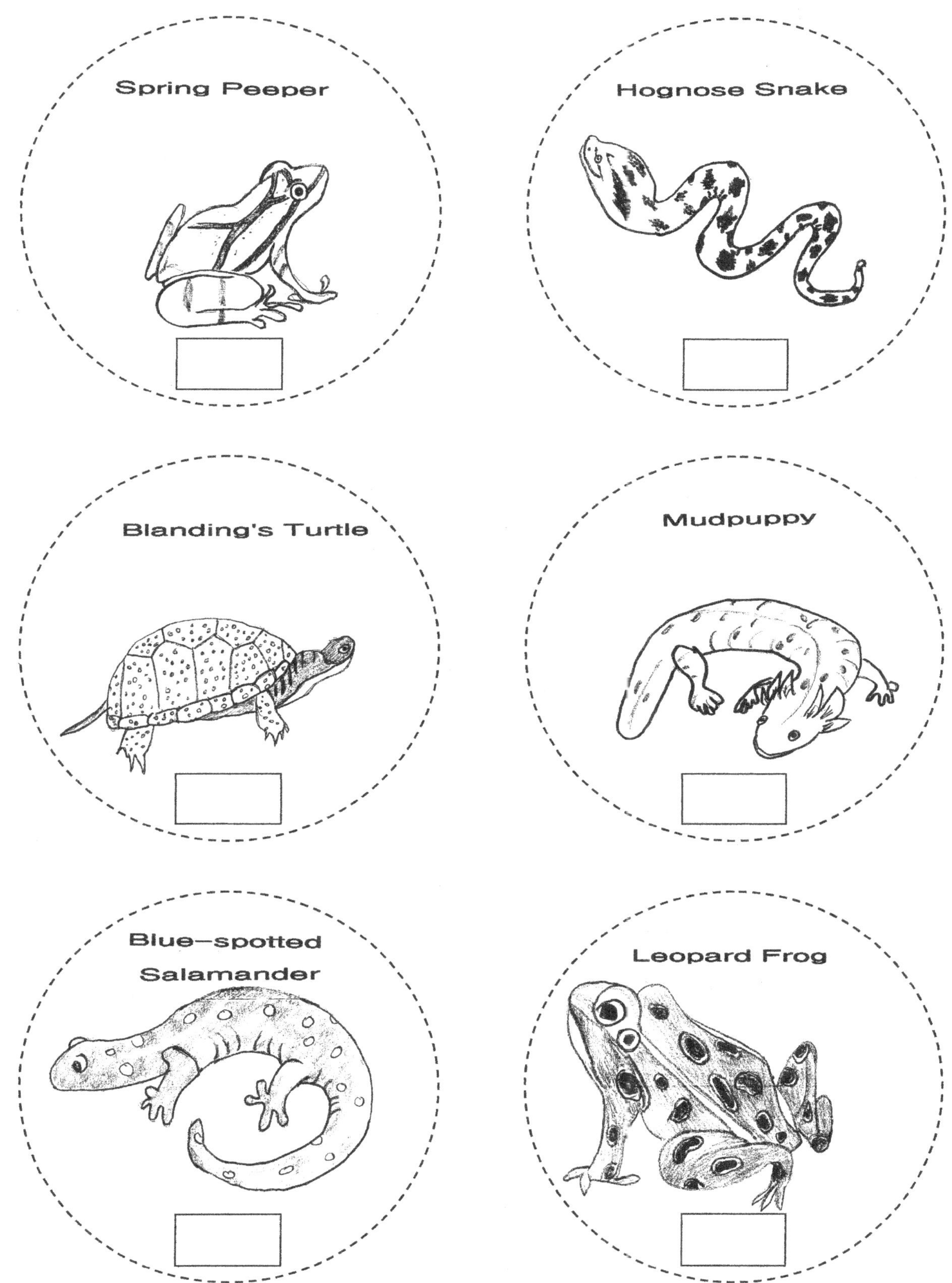

Spring Peeper
Hognose Snake
Blanding's Turtle
Mudpuppy
Blue-spotted Salamander
Leopard Frog

The Amphibians and Reptiles Game		**Name:**	**Points:**
Wood Turtle	Five-lined Skink	Fowler's Toad	Massassauga Rattlesnake
Fox Snake	Road Mortality	Illegal Collector	Red-spotted Newt
Spring Peeper	Habitat Loss	Conservation Officer	Hognose Snake
Blanding's Turtle	Mudpuppy	Blue-spotted Salamander	Leopard Frog

The Amphibians and Reptiles Game		**Name:**	**Points:**
Wood Turtle	Five-lined Skink	Fowler's Toad	Massassauga Rattlesnake
Fox Snake	Road Mortality	Illegal Collector	Red-spotted Newt
Spring Peeper	Habitat Loss	Conservation Officer	Hognose Snake
Blanding's Turtle	Mudpuppy	Blue-spotted Salamander	Leopard Frog

<u>**The Water Form Game**</u>

Ecological Explanation

Water comes in three states: solid, liquid and gas. It comes in many forms. Some of these forms are ice, snow, hail, rain, steam and vapour. Water changes form as it travels through the water cycle. It may rise into the air as water vapour,; form ice in clouds and fall down as rain, to begin the water cycle again. Scientists believe that the same amount of water has existed on the planet for millions and millions of years, and that it never disappears, just changes form. I like to tell children that a water molecule from a T-rex could have gone through the water cycle a few thousand times and exist in their body at the present moment.

The surface of the earth is covered with over two-thirds water. Astronauts recall seeing Planet Earth from outer space, and marveling at the image of a blue ball suspended in black space. Yet even though the surface of the earth is covered with over two-thirds water, about 97% of that water is salty ocean water. Another 2% is tied up in the polar ice caps. In fact, less than one per cent of the world's water is clean and fresh enough for human consumption, and this supply is getting scarcer all the time. Many children who live in North America particularly those who live around the Great Lakes- the largest supply of fresh water in the world- have never even considered that fresh water is scarce. Many simply take fresh water for granted. So the concept of conserving fresh water must be put into a context that they can relate to.

The human body is close to over two-thirds water as well. All living things need water to survive. So understanding that a healthy water supply is directly related to the health of all living things on the planet is essential.

Children will readily tell you that they have seen unsightly garbage and pictures of oil spills in water. They are keen to do something to solve the problem. The Water Form Game helps to introduce all of the above concepts.

Specific Instructions

In the Water Game, students must run around the playing area and search for twelve game signs, each with a picture and name of an insect. When they find a game sign, they write the Morse code symbol in the box on the game card that matches the game sign. The boundary patrollers take on the role of drainpipe. The educator troubleshoots in the game as the Conservation Officer.

Part way through the game, blow the whistle and have students come back to home base. The educator chooses two students to be the limiting factors of oil spill and pollution. The remaining students get two Popsicle sticks, which

each represent a raindrop. Begin the game again and follow the instructions in the Game Format chapter.

Blow the whistle at the end of the game to signal all students to return to home base. Tally up the points. The points on a game card represent the number of water forms that player found and transformed into. The Limiting Factors' Popsicle sticks represent the number of raindrops that came into contact with oil spills and pollution.

Give the students the Morse code alphabet. Students must decode the Morse code alphabet into English letters and then unscramble the letters to find the secret environmental message: SAVE OUR WATER.

Extension and Assessment Suggestions

1) Add this poem to the back of the game card. Children can visually represent their understanding of the poem, or come up with ways to change their habits to try and conserve water.

<u>**Air and Water in the Environment**</u>

There are two things that we all must get:

Air that's pure and water that's wet,

They help us to live every day,

But there's a problem in the way.

Pollution gives me quite a scare,

If it gets in the water and the air.

Smog, oil spills, garbage too,

But there are things that you can do.

Change your habits; use your wit,

And our env ronment will benefit.

So make a plan and stick to it

Because every step helps - Even a little bit.

Jen Baron, June 2001

2) Clean garbage from a river, pond or beach.
3) Sort the water forms on the game card into solid, liquid or gas.

Literacy Links

Base, Graeme. **The Water Hole.** *Doubleday Canada, 2001.*

Greenaway, Theresa. <u>The Water Cycle.</u> Raintree, Steck-Vaughn Publishers, New York, 2001.

Jeunesse, Gallimard and PM Valat. **Water.** Moonlight Publishing, 1991.

Locker, Thomas. **Water Dance.** Harcourt Brace & Company, SanDiego, 1997.

Web Links

www.wwf.org and link to World Ocean's Day.

www.greengames.org for The Water Game.

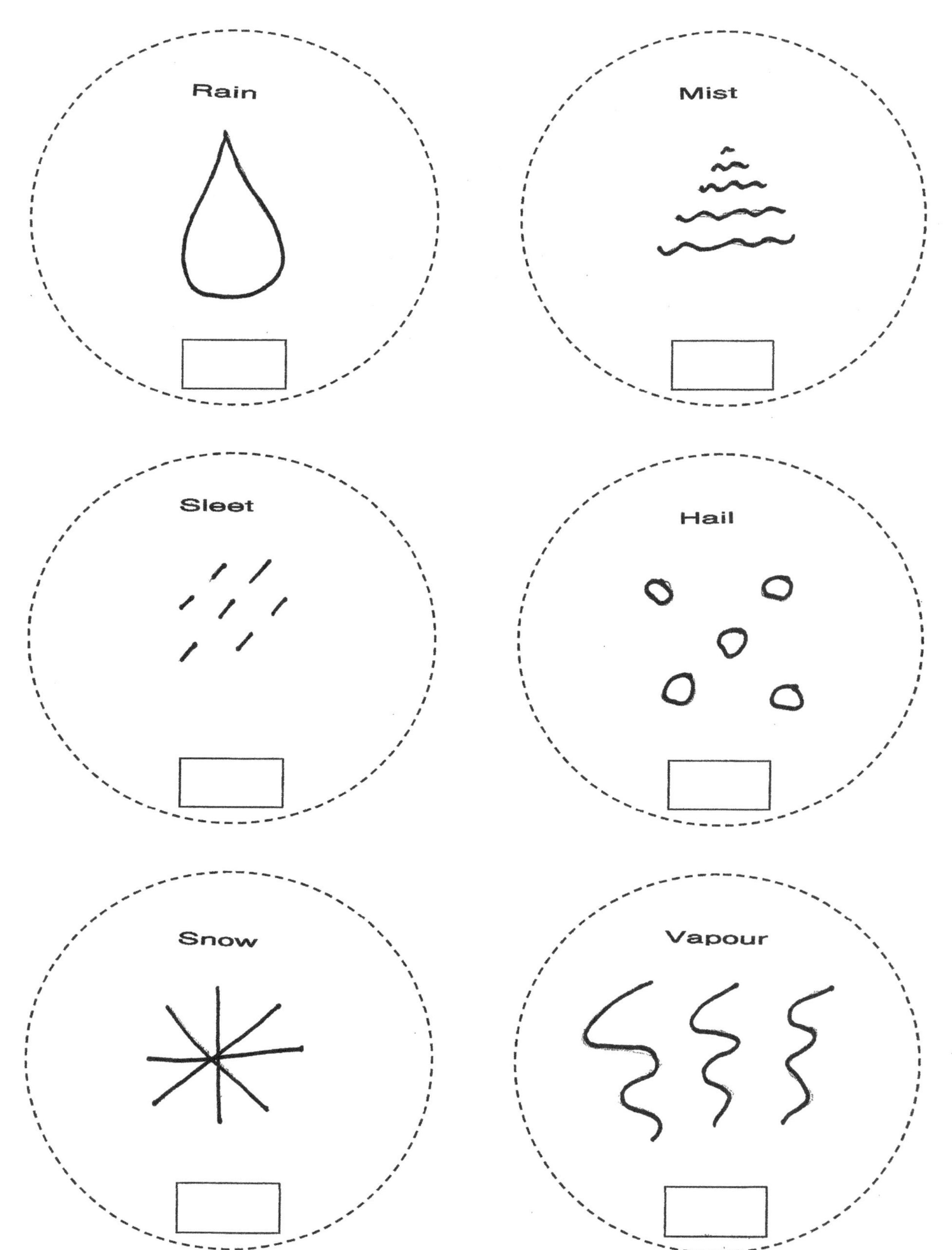

Rain
Mist
Sleet
Hail
Snow
Vapour

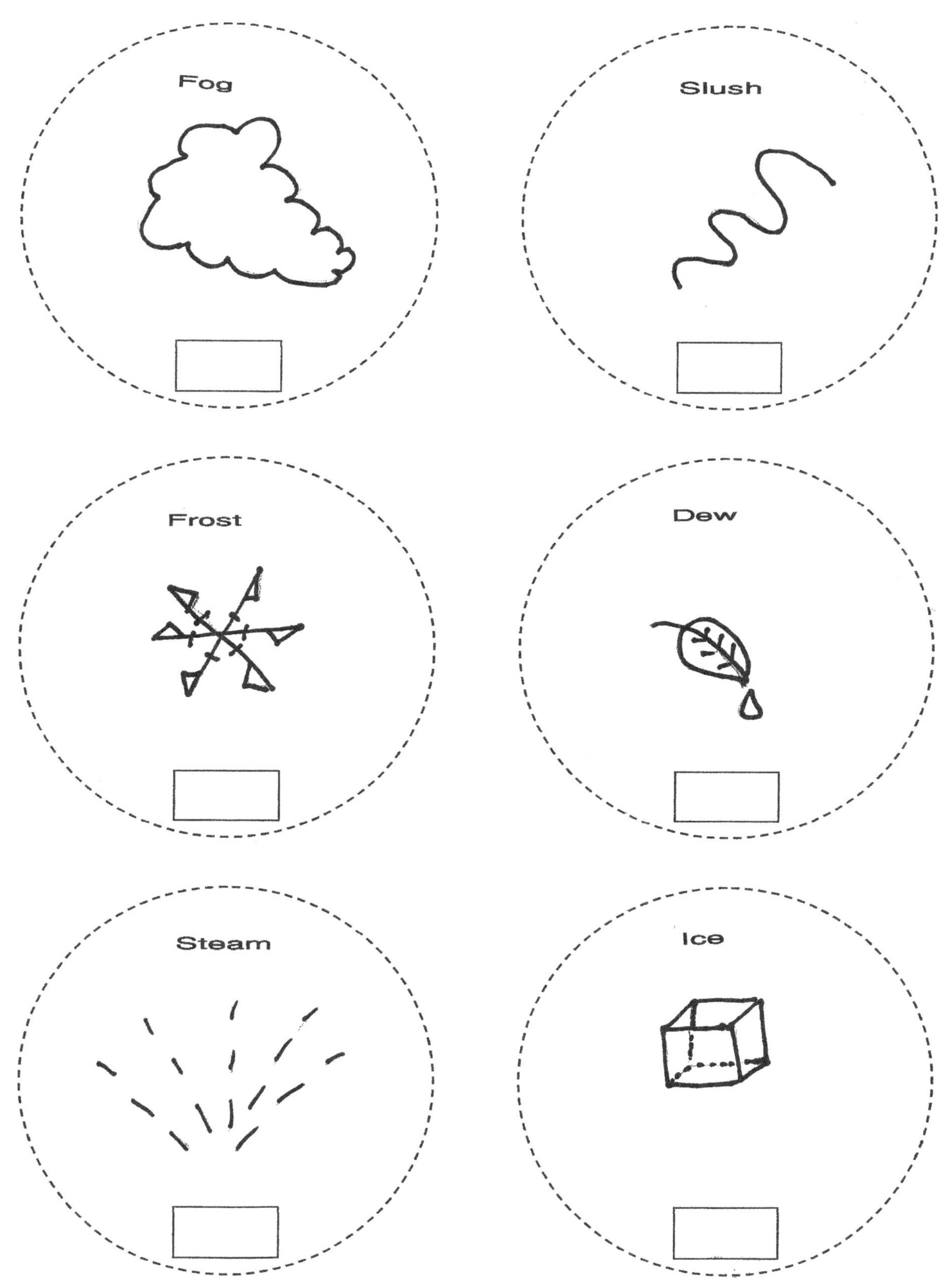
Fog
Slush
Frost
Dew
Steam
Ice

The Water Game		**Name:**	**Points:**
Rain	Mist	Sleet	Hail
Snow	Pollution	Drain Pipe	Vapour
Fog	Oil Spill	Conservation Officer	Slush
Frost	Dew	Steam	Ice

Air and Water in the Environment

There are two things that we all must get:
Air that's pure and water that's wet.
They help us to live every day,
But there's a problem in the way.
Pollution gives me quite a scare,
If it gets in the water and the air.
Smog, oil spills, garbage too,
But there are things that you can do.
Change your habits; use your wit;
And our environment will benefit.
So make a plan and stick to it,
Because every step helps – even a little bit.

Jen Baron, June 2001

The Wildflower Game Instructions

Ecological Explanation

People are universally attracted to the beauty of wildflowers. These plants are an integral part of the ecosystems in which they inhabit. They are able to produce their own food through the chemical process of photosynthesis. In turn, they form the base of all food chains.

Unfortunately, many wildflowers are becoming endangered. The main reason for this is loss of habitat. Many variables contribute to loss of wildflower habitat. The largest factors include habitat loss due to human use of that space for agricultural purposes; road building and residential and industrial development. Some wildflowers are particularly vulnerable to human recreational activity if their habitat is along shorelines, dunes or beaches where people may trample these flowers. Also, wetlands are a storehouse of biodiversity, wildflowers being no exception. Unfortunately, wetlands are disappearing in North America at an alarming rate, and as that leads to a destruction of vital wildflower habitat.

Invading plant species, such as Purple Loosestrife in North America, often have no natural predators in their alien ecosystem. Therefore they thrive at the expense of the indigenous wildflower species. It is very important to have a coordinated effort amongst government, businesses and individuals to ensure that invasive plant species do not spread.

Wildflowers are so pretty that it is possible to love them to death. Pickers, collectors and people who intentionally transplant wildflowers prove harmful to the health of many wildflower species, such as Lady's Slippers. Encourage students to observe, but not pick, wildflowers. Also, in trying to protect wildflowers from pests, gardeners may actually misapply pesticides, causing more damage to the flower than good. Research with students how to use organic gardening practices.

Specific Instructions

In The Wildflower Game, students have to run around the playing area searching for the twelve game signs, which each have a different wildflower picture and name on them. When they find a game sign, they record the Morse code symbol in the box on the game card that matches the wildflower picture and name on the game sign. The boundary patrollers take on the role of collector.

Part way through the game, blow the whistle and have students come back to home base. The educator chooses two students to be the limiting factors of habitat loss and invading species. The remaining students get two Popsicle sticks, which each represent a single wildflower. Begin the game again and follow the instructions in the Game Format chapter.

Blow the whistle at the end of the game to signal all students to return to home base. Tally up the points. The points on a game card represent the number of wildflowers that player saved. The Limiting Factors' Popsicle sticks represent the number of flowers that succumbed to habitat loss and invading species.

Give the students the Morse code alphabet. Students must decode the Morse code alphabet into English letters and then unscramble the letters to find the secret environmental message: PLANT A FLOWER.

Extension Activities and Assessment Suggestions

Students could:

1) plant a wildflower garden in the schoolyard and keep a record of the insects and birds that come to their garden. Discourage use of pesticides and research other tips for an organic gardening approach;
2) research the wildflowers in their local habitat and keep a wildflower log of those they can find.; research their country's provincial or state official flowers and any laws regarding those flowers;
3) observe still life drawings and paintings of flowers, and try their hand at creating their own works of art.

Literature Links

Godkin, Celia. Ladybug Garden. Markham: Fitzhenry & Whiteside, 1995.

Grant, Tim and Gail Littlejohn. Greening School Grounds: Creating Habitats for Learning. British Columbia: New Society Publishers.

Newcomb, Lawrence. Newcomb's Wildflower Guide. New York: Little, Brown and Company, 1977.

Peterson, Roger Tory. Peterson First Guides: Wildflowers. Boston: Houghton Mifflin Company, 1986.

Web Links

www.great-lakes.net
www.kidsgardening.com
www.schoolgrounds.ca

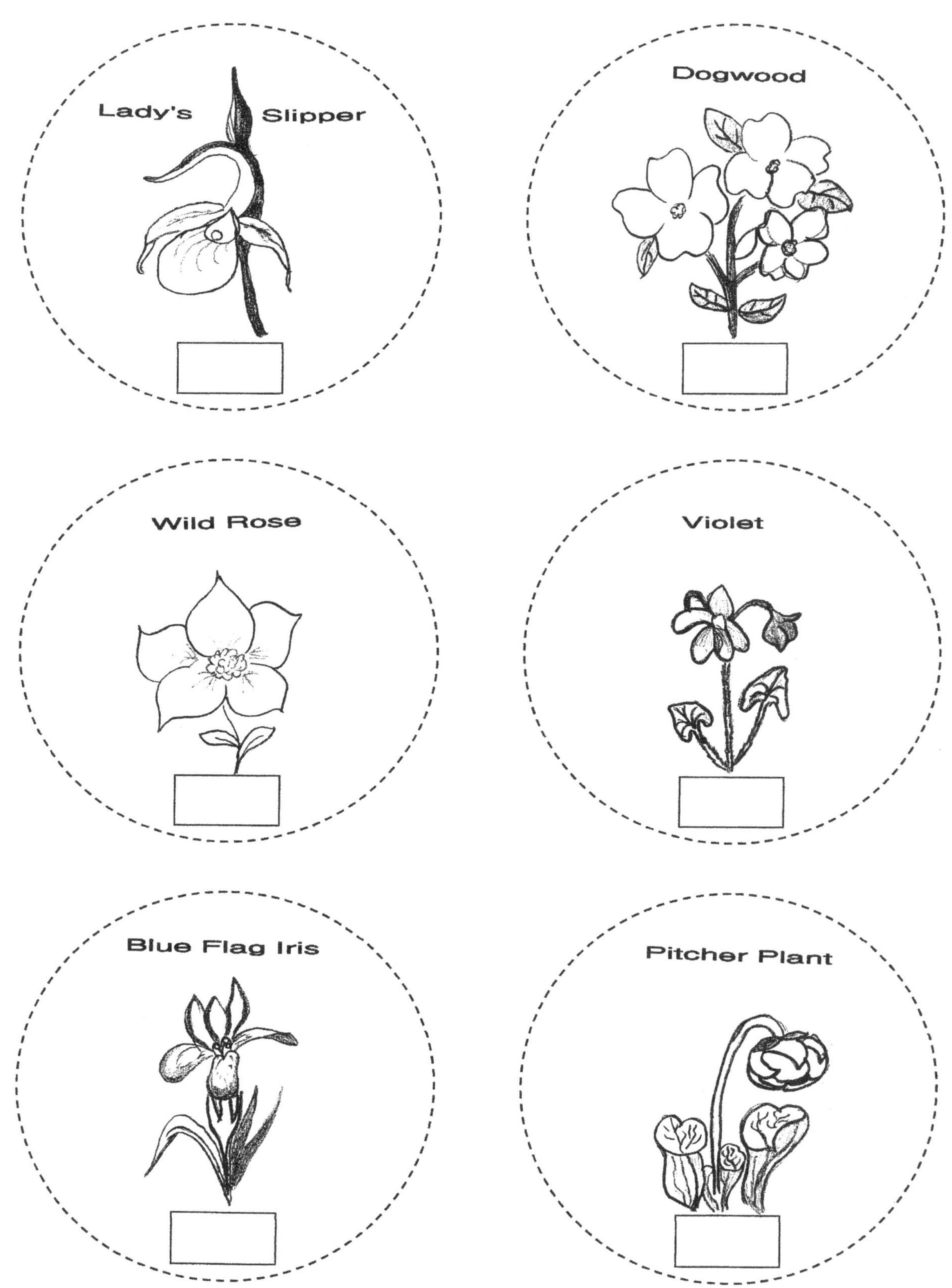

Lady's Slipper
Dogwood
Wild Rose
Violet
Blue Flag Iris
Pitcher Plant

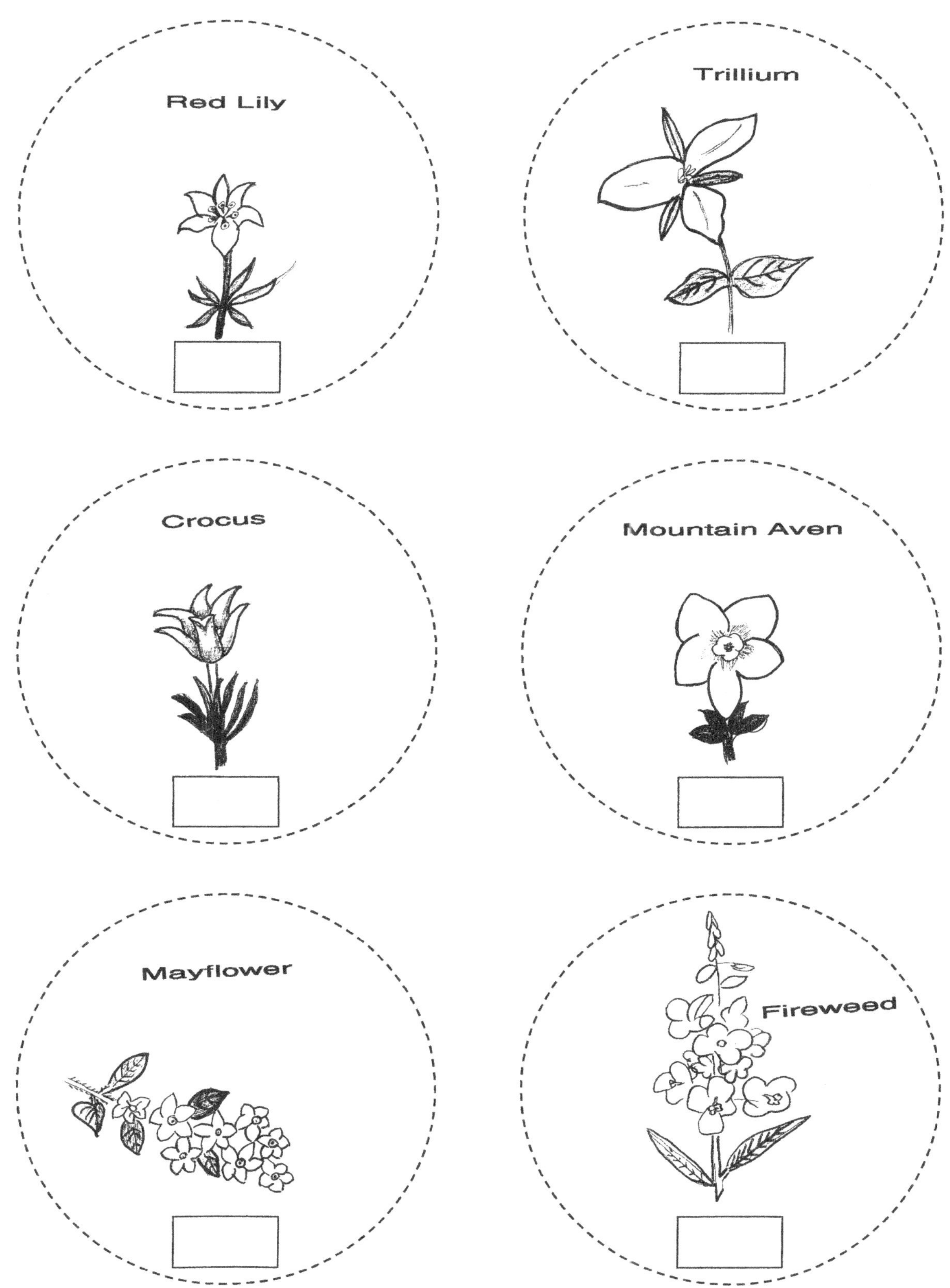

Red Lily
Trillium
Crocus
Mountain Aven
Mayflower
Fireweed

The Wildflower Game		Name:	Points:
Lady's Slipper	Dogwood	Wild Rose	Violet
Blue Flag Iris	Invading Species	Collector	Pitcher Plant
Red Lily	Habitat Loss	Conservation Officer	Trillium
Crocus	Mountain Aven	Mayflower	Fireweed

The Wildflower Game		Name:	Points:
Lady's Slipper	Dogwood	Wild Rose	Violet
Blue Flag Iris	Invading Species	Collector	Pitcher Plant
Red Lily	Habitat Loss	Conservation Officer	Trillium
Crocus	Mountain Aven	Mayflower	Fireweed

The Tree Game

Ecological Explanation

Trees provide so many things for human beings: wood for paper, furniture and buildings; sap for maple syrup, fruit, oxygen and shade on a hot summer's day. Ask any child what the world would be like without trees and he or she would be able to come with a list of very important things that would be missing.

Trees and forests also provide habitat for a wide diversity of animals.

The kind of tree that grows in any given area is dependent upon the specific climactic and growing conditions of that space, such as soil conditions and amount of sunlight. For example, the kind of trees that grow first after a forest fire are very different from the trees found in an old growth climax forest.

In the Forest Game students will be able introduced to identifying the kind of tree with its leaf or needle. In the extension activities, students can take the process one step further by classifying trees according to their leaf and needle appearance and structure.

Forest fires caused by events in nature, such as severe thunderstorms with lighting, have been a part of the natural evolution of forests since they began. However, today careless individuals who may leave a campfire burning, discard glass or a lit cigarette or match are the cause of damaging forest fires throughout North America every year. Although fires play an important role in forest succession, it is also imperative that people try not to be careless in starting a fire that can destroy and damage plant, animal and human habitat and life.

Trees provided essential resources for people and have done so for thousands of years. There was obviously a time when people were using trees at a sustainable level. In recent history, this is most certainly not the case. People across the globe are deforesting their countries at such a rapid rate that it is considered a major cause in the trend towards desertification and perhaps even global warming.

The method of clear cutting forests has far-reaching ecological effects including soil erosion, loss of habitat for animals and in some cases species extinction. It is important to search for alternatives to clear cutting forest as a method of tree harvesting.

Specific Instructions

In the Tree Game, students must run around the playing area and search for twelve game signs, each with a picture and name of a tree. When they find a game sign, they write the Morse code symbol in the box on the game card that matches the game sign. The boundary patrollers take on the role of lake. The educator troubleshoots in the game as the forest biologist.

Part way through the game, blow the whistle and have students come back to home base. The educator chooses two students to be the limiting factors of forest fires and clear cuts. The remaining students get two Popsicle sticks, which each represent a single tree. Begin the game again and follow the instructions in the Game Format chapter.

Blow the whistle at the end of the game to signal all students to return to home base. Tally up the points. The points on a game card represent the number of trees that player saved. The Limiting Factors' Popsicles represents the number of insects that succumbed to forest fires and clear cuts.

Give the students the Morse code alphabet. Students must decode the Morse code alphabet into English letters and then unscramble the letters to find the secret environmental message: PREVENT FIRES.

Extension and Assessment Activities

Students could:

1) brainstorm and record all of the benefits and resources from trees;
2) view artists' images of trees and create their own;
3) research classification systems of trees and create their own;
4) research logging methods and debate which one they feel is best.

Literacy Links

Dr. Suess. <u>The Lorax</u>. New York: Random House Inc., 1971.

Focus on Forests

Krupinski, Loretta: <u>Into the woods: a woodland scrapbook</u>. USA: 1997

Silverstein, Shel. <u>The Giving Tree.</u> USA: Harper Collins Publishers, 1964.

Taylor, Kim. <u>Forest Life.</u> London: Dorling Kindersley Ltd., 1993.

Web Links

www.clearcutnovascotia.com
www.lowimpactforestry.com
www.smokeybear.com

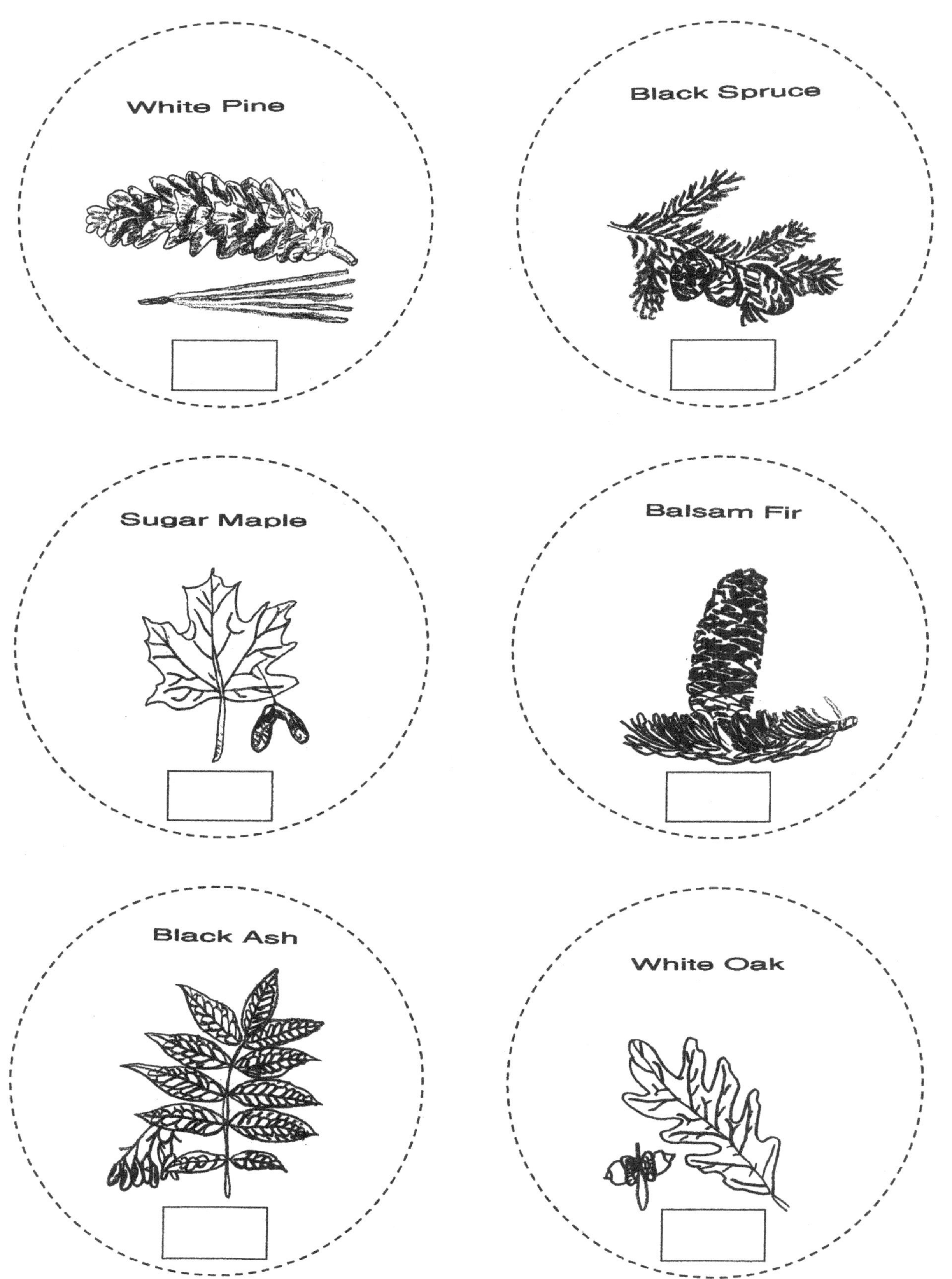

White Pine
Black Spruce
Sugar Maple
Balsam Fir
Black Ash
White Oak

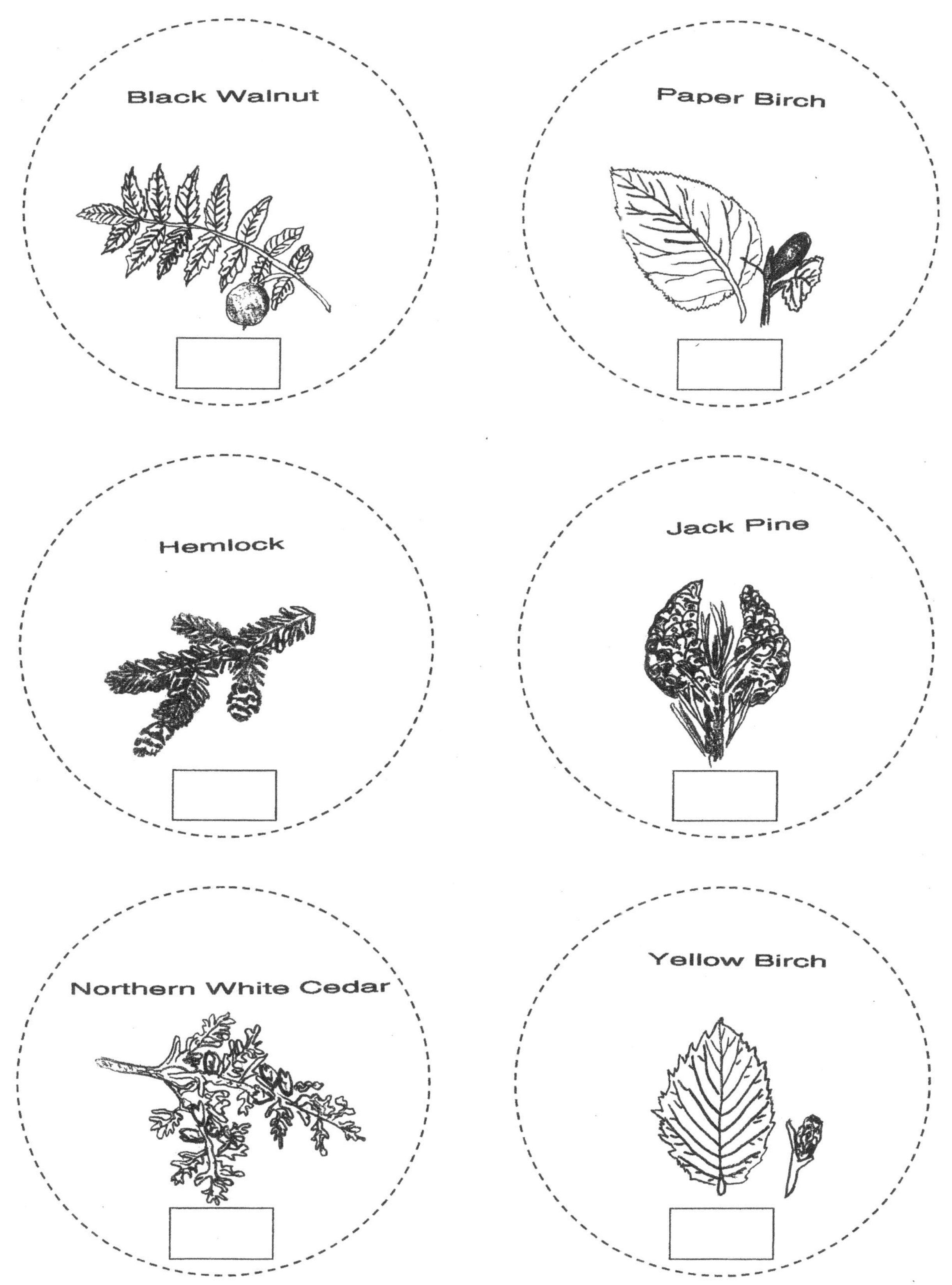

Black Walnut
Paper Birch
Hemlock
Jack Pine
Northern White Cedar
Yellow Birch

The Tree Game		Name:	Points:
White Pine 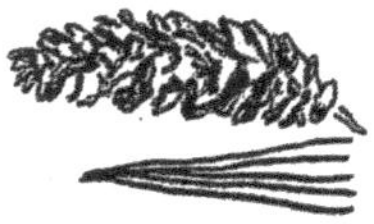	Black Spruce 	Sugar Maple 	Balsam Fir 
Black Walnut 	Clear Cut	Lake	Paper Birch 
Hemlock 	Forest fire	Forester	Jack Pine 
Northern White Cedar 	Yellow Birch 	Black Ash 	White Oak 

The Tree Game		Name:	Points:
White Pine 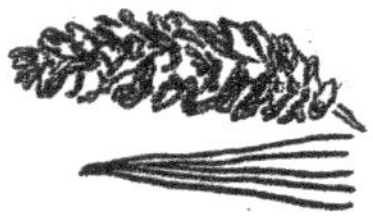	Black Spruce 	Sugar Maple 	Balsam Fir 
Black Walnut 	Clear Cut	Lake	Paper Birch 
Hemlock 	Forest fire	Forester	Jack Pine 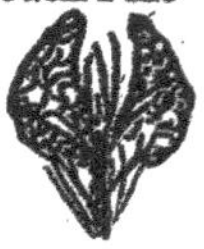
Northern White Cedar 	Yellow Birch 	Black Ash 	White Oak 

The Ocean Game

Ecological Explanation

The oceans cover the vast majority of our planet Earth. Children are innately fascinated with ocean animals, particularly the largest mammals in the world, whales. Even small tidal pools will hold a child's enraptured attention as she peers down into it and observes sea urchins, anemones and starfish. They delight at sightings and pictures of fanciful seahorses, octopus and jellyfish. And, of course, they are filled with awestruck trepidation at the wide variety of sharks that live in the oceans.

Children are fascinated by the food webs in the ocean and many works of fiction are built upon this age-old fascination, most recently told in the blockbuster film, *Finding Nemo.*

Many children I have spoken to feel saddened and at a loss of what to do when they see images of animals covered in oil after an oil spill in the ocean. I have been surprised by how many children are aware of this particular issue and how strongly it effects their sense of injustice. Seabirds that bob along the surface of the ocean are so greatly affected by oil spills. Even a small amount of oil on a bird's feathers can cause the bird damage to its ability to insulate itself, and it can die.

Children are also deeply saddened to learn of the endangered status of so many of the world's whales. They feel a strong sense of loss when they learn of the fact that human overfishing in recent history has lead to the decline of so many ocean species.

For many students, actually visiting a real ocean is not a possibility as a field trip. Yet, children feel a strong connection to oceans. And the issues befalling our world's ocean animals are incredibly significant. It is therefore important to cover ocean ecosystems, even if it not in one's community. The Ocean Game provides a way to introduce fascinating ocean animals and serious issues effecting these animals in a way that will not overwhelm students. The suggested activities and information in the web sites provide ideas for students to get involved, direct their energy based upon their concerns, and create a difference for ocean animals in the future.

Specific Instructions

In The Ocean Game, students have to run around the playing area searching for the twelve game signs, which each have a different ocean animal picture and name on them. When they find a game sign, they record the Morse code symbol in the box on the game card that matches the ocean animal picture and name on the game sign. The boundary patrollers take on the role of dragnet. The teacher is the troubleshooter in the game, as Marine Biologist.

Part way through the game, blow the whistle and have students come back to home base. The educator chooses two students to be the limiting factors of overfishing and pollution. The remaining students get two Popsicle sticks, which each represent an ocean animal. Begin the game again and follow the instructions in the Game Format chapter.

Blow the whistle at the end of the game to signal all students to return to home base. Tally up the points. The points on a game card represent the number of ocean animals that player saved. The Limiting Factors' popsicles represents the number of birds that succumbed overfishing and pollution.

Give the students the Morse code alphabet. Students must decode the Morse code alphabet into English letters and then unscramble the letters to find the secret environmental message: SAVE OUR SEAS!

Extension Activities and Assessment Suggestions

1) Students could research an ocean ecosystem and represent in a work of art, such as an "Under the Sea" diorama, mural or painting. Water colour paint over wax crayons or oil pastels work well.
2) Many birds that use freshwater habitats also live in ocean habitats, such as loons and herons. By cleaning up garbage from a pond, river, beach or seashore, one is helping these birds.
3) Fundraise for organizations that have specific ocean ecosystem projects, such as World Wildlife Fund.

Literacy Story

Baker, Alan. Look Who Lives In the Ocean. Great Britain: Macdonald Young Books, 1998.

Hickman, Pamela. See, Make and Do: At The Seashore. Halifax, Nova Scotia: Formac Publishing Co. Ltd., 1996.

Tibbits, Christiane Kump. Take-Along-Guide: Seashells, Crabs and Seastars. Northwood Press: Chanhasses, MN, 1996.

Web Links

www.wwf.org and link to World Ocean's Day.

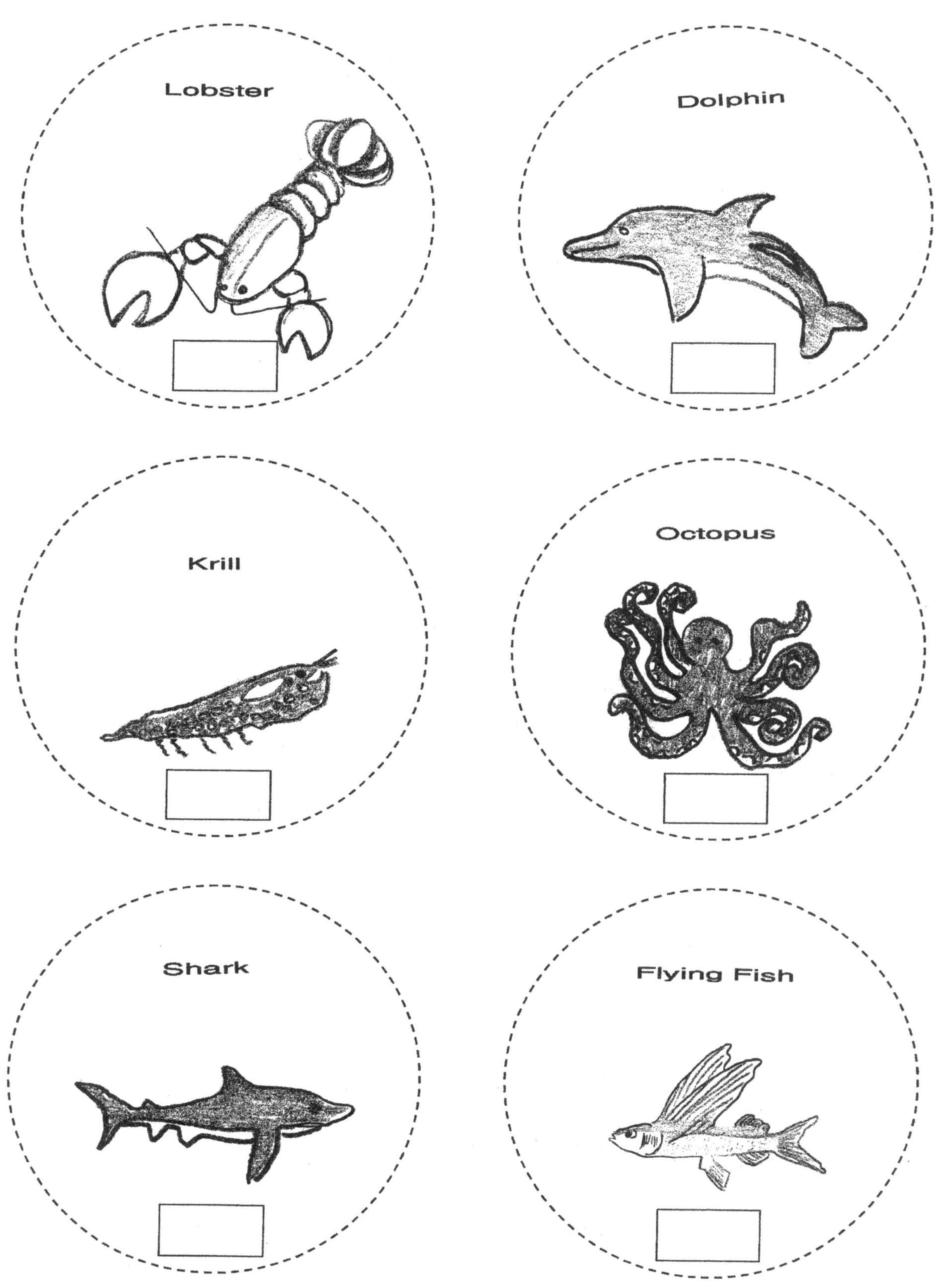

Lobster
Dolphin
Krill
Octopus
Shark
Flying Fish

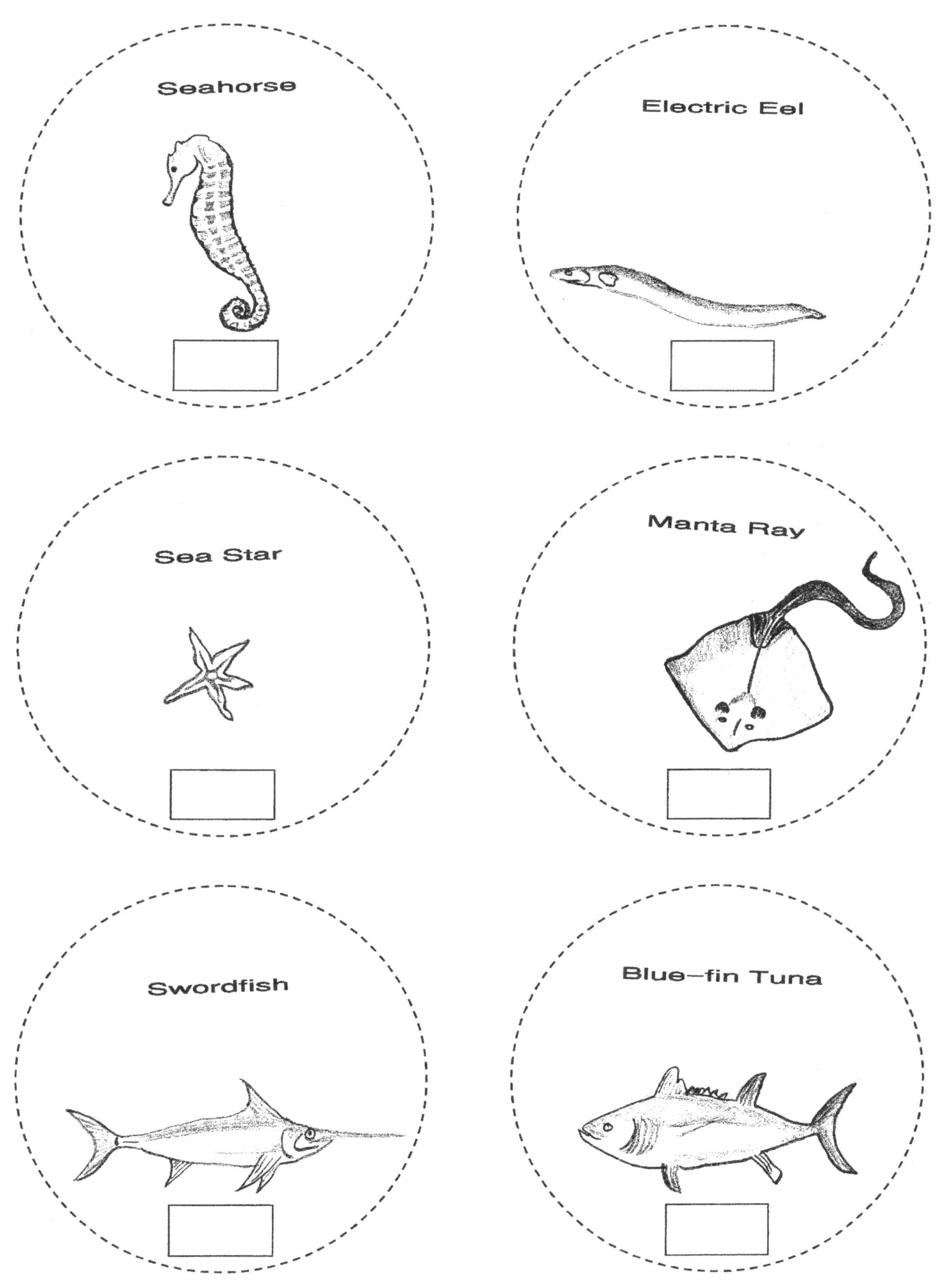

Seahorse
Electric Eel
Sea Star
Manta Ray
Swordfish
Blue-fin Tuna

The Ocean Game		Name:	Points:
Lobster 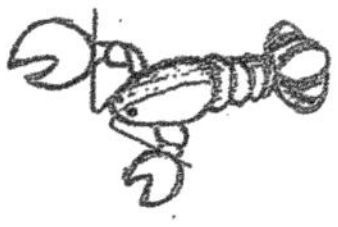	Dolphin 	Krill 	Octopus 
Shark 	Over-fishing	Dragnet	Flying Fish 
Seahorse 	Pollution	Marine Biologist	Electric Eel 
Sea Star 	Manta Ray 	Blue-fin Tuna 	Swordfish 

The Ocean Game		Name:	Points:
Lobster 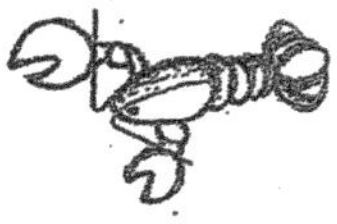	Dolphin 	Krill 	Octopus 
Shark 	Over-fishing	Dragnet	Flying Fish 
Seahorse 	Pollution	Marine Biologist	Electric Eel 
Sea Star 	Manta Ray 	Blue-fin Tuna 	Swordfish 

The Rock Cycle Game

Ecological Explanation

A rock is composed of two or more minerals. Minerals are made up of an orderly arrangement of atoms with a definite internal structure and consistent composition. All rocks can be placed into one of three groups: igneous, sedimentary and metamorphic. The processes which effect the formation and development of rocks are known together as the rock cycle.

Igneous rocks come from cooled magma. Rocks that come from magma which has cooled quickly outside of the earth's crust are called extrusive igneous rocks, such as obsidian. Magma that has had a longer time to cool and form larger crystals inside of the earth's crust is called intrusive igneous rock, such as granite.

Weathering alters rocks. This weathering process is known as erosion. It will cause igneous rocks to decay, crumble and loose debris, such as clay, sand and gravel. Eventually, these sediments form layers, as process known as lithification. These sediments become compacted, cemented and recrystallize. Over time they harden slowly into sedimentary rocks. Examples of sedimentary rock are sandstone, siltstone, shale and conglomerate. Organic materials that decompose, form layers and harden also form sedimentary rocks, such as limestone and coal.

Temperature and pressure will change the composition, texture and internal structure of sedimentary rocks. This process is called metamorphism. Examples of metamorphic rocks are: gneiss, schist and marble.

When metamorphic rocks melt and form new magma, the cycle has come full circle. The rock cycle may take millions and billions of years to complete, or it may be interrupted at various stages through the action of a particular process. For example, igneous or sedimentary rocks may melt in a volcanic eruption to form new magma.

Although the rock cycle is a continuous process, rocks and minerals are formed over millions of years. Therefore, rocks and minerals are considered to be a non-renewable resource. Resource extraction, like mining, removes the mineral and rocks from the earth where it took specific conditions and long periods of time to create them. In this game, students will see that erosion and mining are limiting factors in the rock cycle.

Specific Instructions

In The Rock Cycle Game, students have to run around the playing area searching for the twelve game signs, which each have a different rock type and symbol on them. When they find a game sign, they record the Morse code symbol in the box on the game card that matches the rock type and symbol on the game sign. The boundary patrollers take on the role of magma.

Part way through the game, blow the whistle and have students come back to home base. The educator chooses two students to be the limiting factors of erosion and mining. The remaining students get two Popsicle sticks, which each represent a single rock. Begin the game again and follow the instructions in the Game Format chapter.

Blow the whistle at the end of the game to signal all students to return to home base. Tally up the points. The points on a game card represent the number of birds that player saved. The Limiting Factors' popsicles represents the number of rocks that succumbed to erosion and mining.

Give the students the Morse code alphabet. Students must decode the Morse code alphabet into English letters and then unscramble the letters to find the secret environmental message: COLLECT ROCKS.

Extension Activities and Assessment Suggestions

1) Classify the rocks on the game card into igneous, sedimentary and metamorphic.
2) Research the geological symbols on the game card. Investigate if there are other geological symbols.
3) Start a rock collection and try to classify their own rocks into the three categories.
4) Research methods geologists use to identify rocks, such as the scratch test.
5) Research the industrial and commercial uses of rocks.
6) Research mining projects in their area.

Literatures Links

Baylor, Byrd. <u>Everybody Needs a Rock.</u> New York: Simon & Schuster, 1974.

<u>ROCK ONtario.</u> Ontario Ministry of Northern Development and Mines. Queen's Printer for Ontario, 1994.

Web Links

www.edselect.com
www.ontariogeoscience.net
www.simplyscience.com

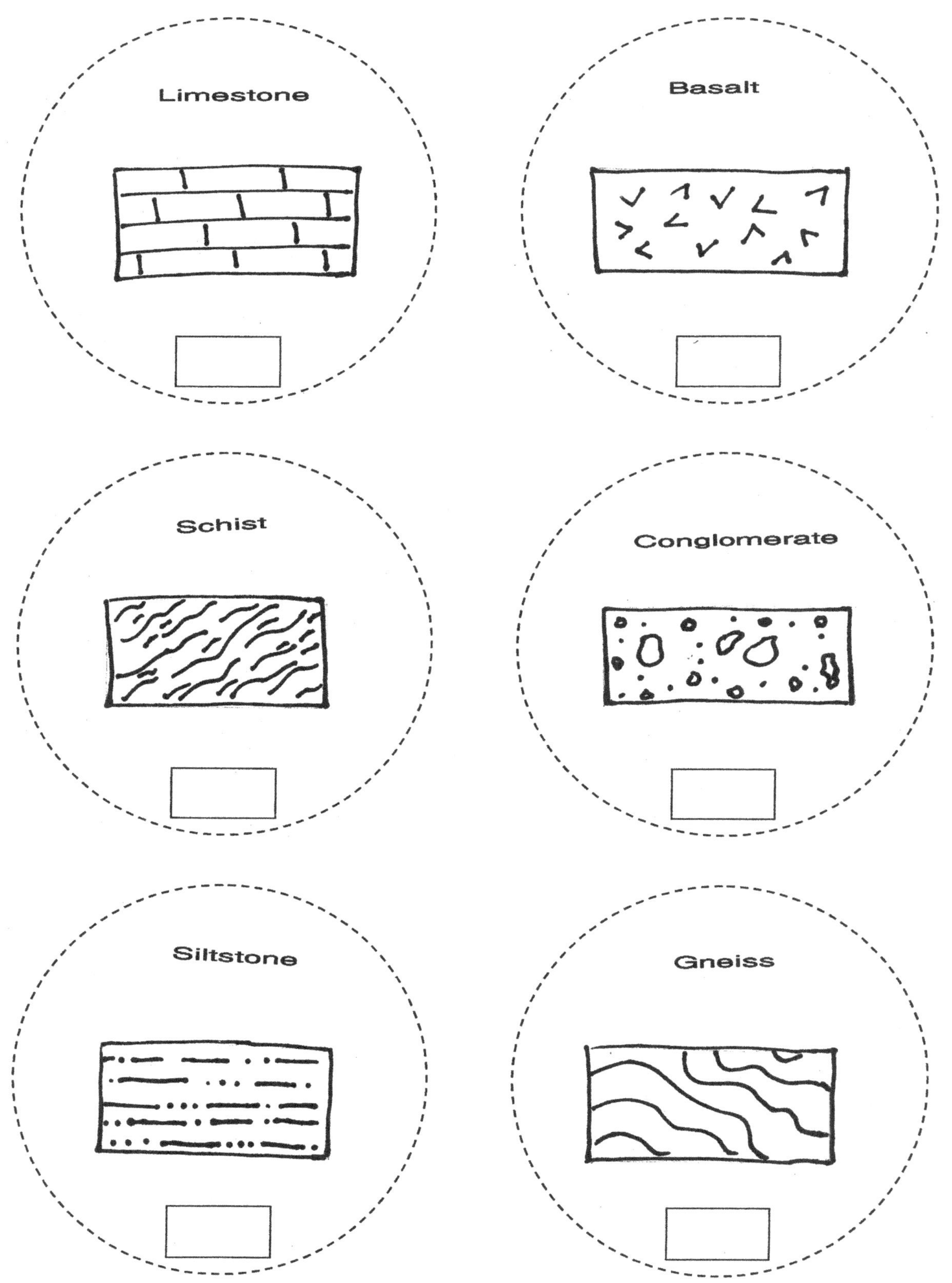

Limestone
Basalt
Schist
Conglomerate
Siltstone
Gneiss

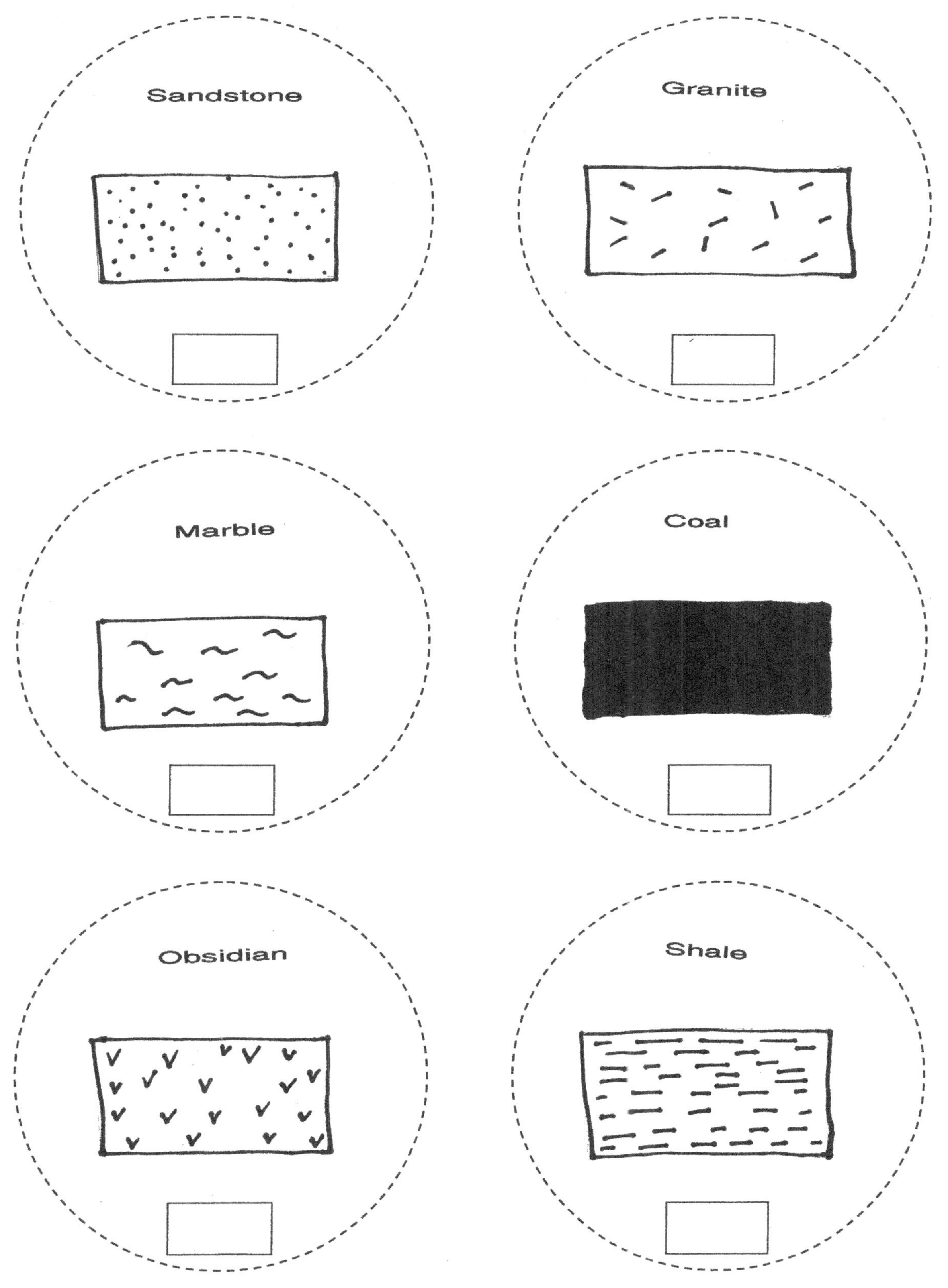

Sandstone
Granite
Marble
Coal
Obsidian
Shale

The Rock Cycle Game		**Name:**	**Points:**
Limestone 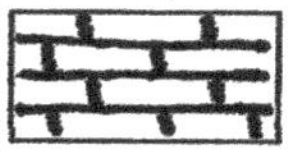	Basalt 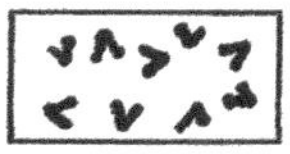	Schist 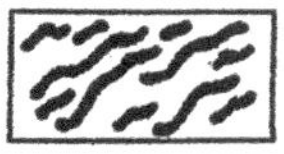	Conglomerate 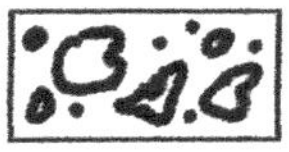
Siltstone	Mining	Magma	Gneiss 
Sandstone 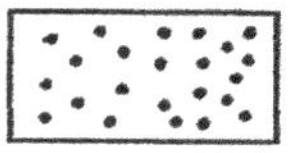	Erosion	Geologist	Granite 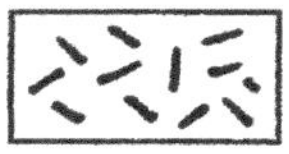
Marble 	Coal 	Obsidian 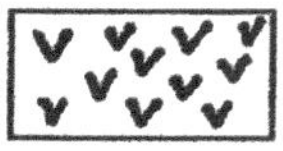	Shale 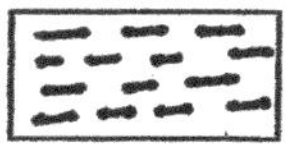

The Rock Cycle Game		**Name:**	**Points:**
Limestone 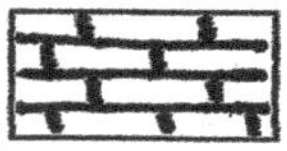	Basalt 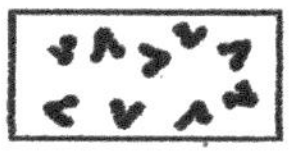	Schist 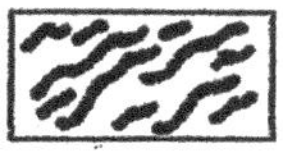	Conglomerate 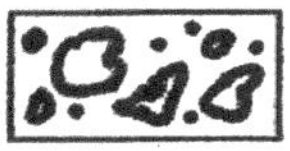
Siltstone	Mining	Magma	Gneiss 
Sandstone 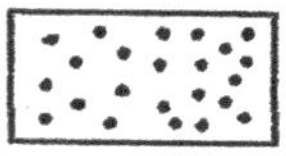	Erosion	Geologist	Granite 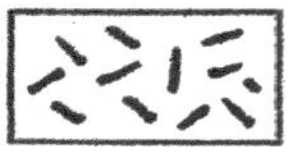
Marble 	Coal	Obsidian 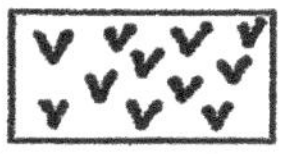	Shale 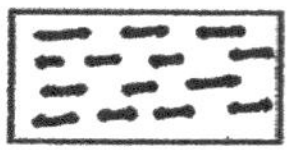

<u>**The Endangered Species Game**</u>

Ecological Explanation

Ask any child to name an animal that has gone extinct, and the answer will most like be "dinosaurs". Some children will even be able to explain the widely accepted theory that meteors struck the earth, perhaps changing the climate so rapidly that dinosaurs were unable to adapt and disappeared from the Earth forever.

In present times, there is another mass extinction of species occurring on planet Earth. Though this time the three main reasons are all linked to human causation: over hunting, pollution and habitat loss. Educators can easily demonstrate the significant effects of species loss by taking a ball of string and starting at one student who names an animal. Another student somewhere else in the room gets the string when he or she can name an animal that eats, or gets eaten by, the first animal. Continue the process and make a food web in the classroom. Now take away an animal due to extinction. Watch the web fall apart.

When children learn about endangered species, they can become disheartened very quickly. The reason for this is that children are very attracted to and interested in animals: they innately care about them and are fascinated by them. To find that people before them have lead to their demise can strike anger, fear and dejection into the emotional energy of youth.

Educators need to direct this powerful learning experience and energy into positive directions. The Endangered Species Game introduces the topic of endangered animals, and the current reasons for their endangerment, in a format that allows students to learn in an engaging and empowering experience.

Students need to be made aware of the positive impacts that youth are having all over the world with their own environmental initiative projects. Now is the time to seize the opportunity to harness the emotional energy that stems from children and youth caring about animals, and do something. Show kids the way to making a difference on our planet.

The Literacy Looks contain books that introduce the reasons for the extinction of animals today and offer some positive courses of action for students to take. The Web Links are about youth environmental leadership and initiatives.

Specific Expectations

In The Endangered Species Game, students have to run around the playing area searching for the twelve game signs, which each have a different endangered species picture and name on them. When they find a game sign, they record the Morse code symbol in the box on the game card that matches the

endangered animal picture and name on the game sign. The boundary patrollers take on the role of poachers. The teacher is the troubleshooter in the game, as Conservation Officer.

Part way through the game, blow the whistle and have students come back to home base. The educator chooses two students to be the limiting factors of habitat loss and pollution. The remaining students get two Popsicle sticks, which each represent an endangered animal. Begin the game again and follow the instructions in the Game Format chapter.

Blow the whistle at the end of the game to signal all students to return to home base. Tally up the points. The points on a game card represent the number of animals that player saved. The Limiting Factors' Popsicles represents the number of endangered animals that succumbed to habitat loss and pollution.

Give the students the Morse code alphabet. Students must decode the Morse code alphabet into English letters and then unscramble the letters to find the secret environmental message: CARE TO CHANGE.

Extension and Assessment Suggestions
Students could:
1) research information about an endangered species and present it in a multi-media format to the class;
2) rehabilitate a habitat in their school yard or local community;
3) fundraise and donate to an organization that works to save endangered species;
4) research laws at all levels of government that are designed to help animals and their habitats.

Literacy Links

Beazley, Karen. <u>Politics of the wild: Canada and endangered species</u>. Don Mills: Oxford University Press, 2001.
<u>Canadian Endangered Species</u>
Gilders, Michelle. <u>Why am I Rare?</u> Calgary: Red Deer Press, 2002.
Godkin, Celia. <u>Sea Otter Inlet.</u> Markham: Fitzhenry & Whiteside, 1997.

Web Links
www.wwf.org
www.skyfishproject.org
www.kidsturncentra_.com
www.timeforkids.com
www.spiritbearyouth.com Spirit Bear Youth organization is the largest youth led environmental organization in the world, with over 5 million members world wide. It's mission is to save the habitat of the Kermode, or Spirit, Bear: a white bear that lives in interior British Columbia. Simon Jackson started the project as a teen.

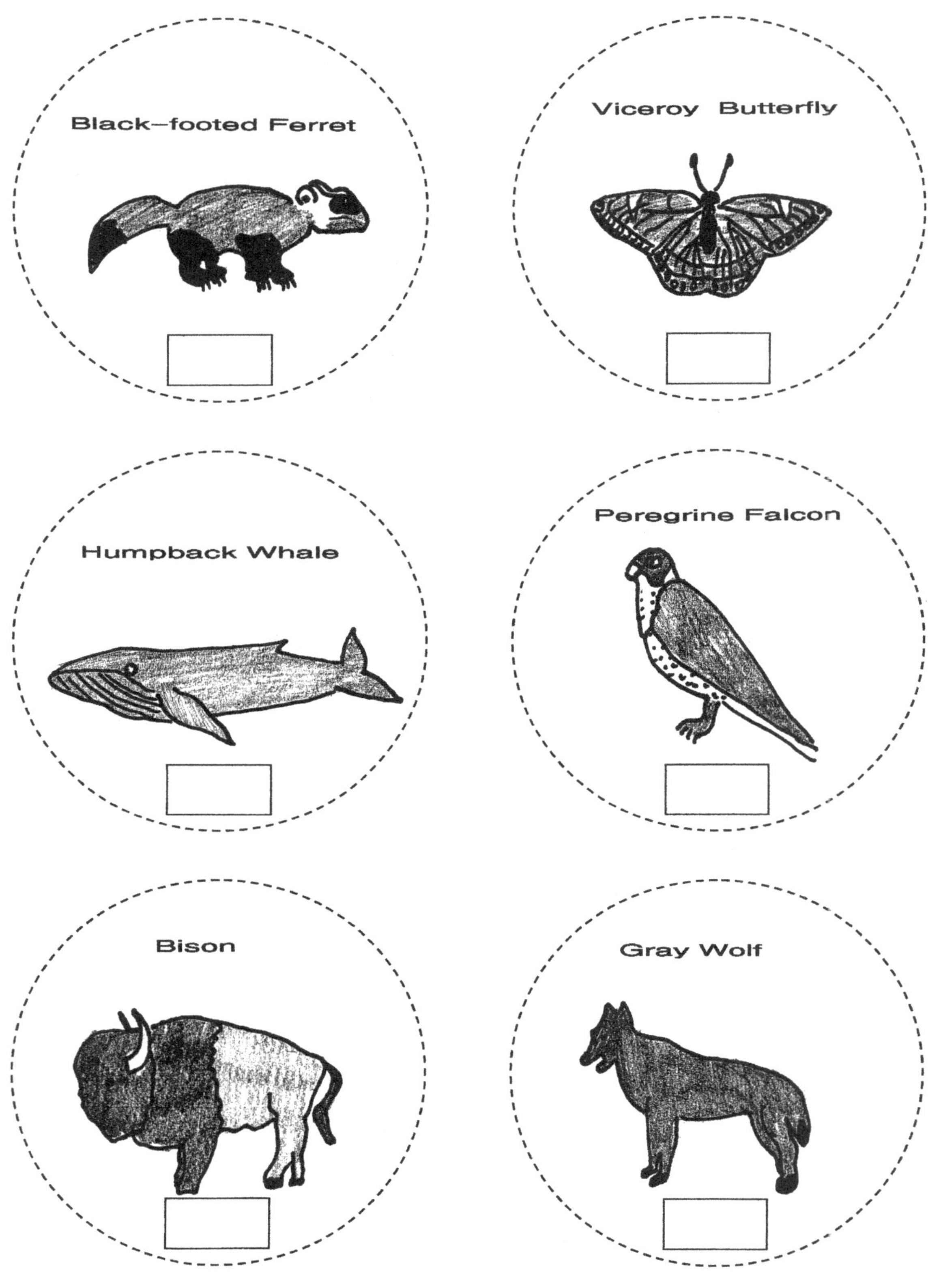

Black—footed Ferret
Viceroy Butterfly
Humpback Whale
Peregrine Falcon
Bison
Gray Wolf

Bald Eagle
Loggerhead
Turtle
River Otter
Grizzly Bear
Spotted Owl
Rattlesnake

The Endangered Species Game		**Name:**	**Points:**
Black-footed Ferret	Viceroy Butterfly	Humpback Whale	Peregrine Falcon
Bison	Pollution	Poacher	Gray Wolf
Bald Eagle	Habitat Loss	Conservation Officer	Loggerhead Turtle
River Otter	Grizzly Bear	Spotted Owl	Rattlesnake

The Endangered Species Game		**Name:**	**Points:**
Black-footed Ferret	Viceroy Butterfly	Humpback Whale	Peregrine Falcon
Bison	Pollution	Poacher	Gray Wolf
Bald Eagle	Habitat Loss	Conservation Officer	Loggerhead Turtle
River Otter	Grizzly Bear	Spotted Owl	Rattlesnake

The Energy Game

Ecological Explanation

People have always used external sources of energy to meet their needs, such as warmth. However, since the industrial revolution people have been using more energy than at any other time in the history of humankind on Earth.

Energy comes from many different sources. People have to retrieve the energy source and convert it into whichever desired form is most suitable, such as electricity or light. All sources of energy have positive and negative aspects to them. For example, wind energy results in very low levels of pollution; however, wind can by nature be inconsistent.

Over the last one hundred and fifty years people have been burning fossil fuels such as coal and oil because they have been relatively accessible, abundant and cheap. Now people realize that these sources of energy cause significant levels of pollution upon combustion., such as smog and acid rain. They also release greenhouse gases, which are associated with global warming. Scientists have made it quite clear that the accessibility of fossil fuels will become more costly and inefficient to retrieve. Ultimately, the use of fossil fuels will reach its end as they are found in finite supply on the planet.

Although many believe that nuclear energy is the answer to solving people's insatiable need for energy, this energy source produces radioactive waste at many stages along the path to being converted into an energy form that people can use, such as electricity.

People often use energy very inefficiently, particularly in heavily industrialized nations such as Canada and the United States. This waste of energy can occur when people leave a light on or a car running. It can also occur when energy is being converted from its source, such as gas, to its form, such as kinetic energy. Heat energy is always released into the atmosphere during inefficient uses of energy. Perhaps the greatest solution to the energy problem is simply to conserve it, and use it as efficiently as possible. For ways to do this, visit David Suzuki's Nature Challenge listed in the Web Links section.

The sources of energy on the game card have value attached to them. This value is based upon how much they pollute. Sources of energy that have relatively low levels of pollution associated with them have higher points.

Educators may wish to change the scoring system based upon their own criteria.

Specific Instructions

In the Energy Game, students must run around the playing area and search for twelve game signs, each with a symbol and name of an energy source. When they find a game sign, they write the Morse code symbol in the box on the game card that matches the game sign. The boundary patrollers take on the role of escaped heat. The educator troubleshoots in the game as the power plant manager.

Part way through the game, blow the whistle and have students come back to home base. The educator chooses two students to be the limiting factors of acid rain and global warming. The remaining students get two Popsicle sticks, which each represent a single source of energy. Begin the game again and follow the instructions in the Game Format chapter.

Blow the whistle at the end of the game to signal all students to return to home base. Tally up the points. The points on a game card represent the number of sources that player conserved. The Limiting Factors' Popsicle sticks represent the number of sources of energy that contributed to global warming and acid rain

Give the students the Morse code alphabet. Students must decode the Morse code alphabet into English letters and then unscramble the letters to find the secret environmental message: CONSERVE HEAT.

Extension and Assessment Suggestions

Students could:
1) Research the positive and negative aspects to the twelve forms of energy on the game card;
2) Do an energy audit at home or school;
3) Brainstorm ways to conserve energy;
4) Research technological advances in alternate energy sources and devices and present their research to the class.

Literature Links

Bang, Molly. <u>My Light</u>.

<u>Teaching About Climate Change</u> Eds. Tim Grant & Gail Littlejohn. BC: New Society Publishers. (Also use with Carbon Cycle Game).

Web Links

www.onetonnechallenge.ca
www.davidsuzuki.org
www.solarenergy.org

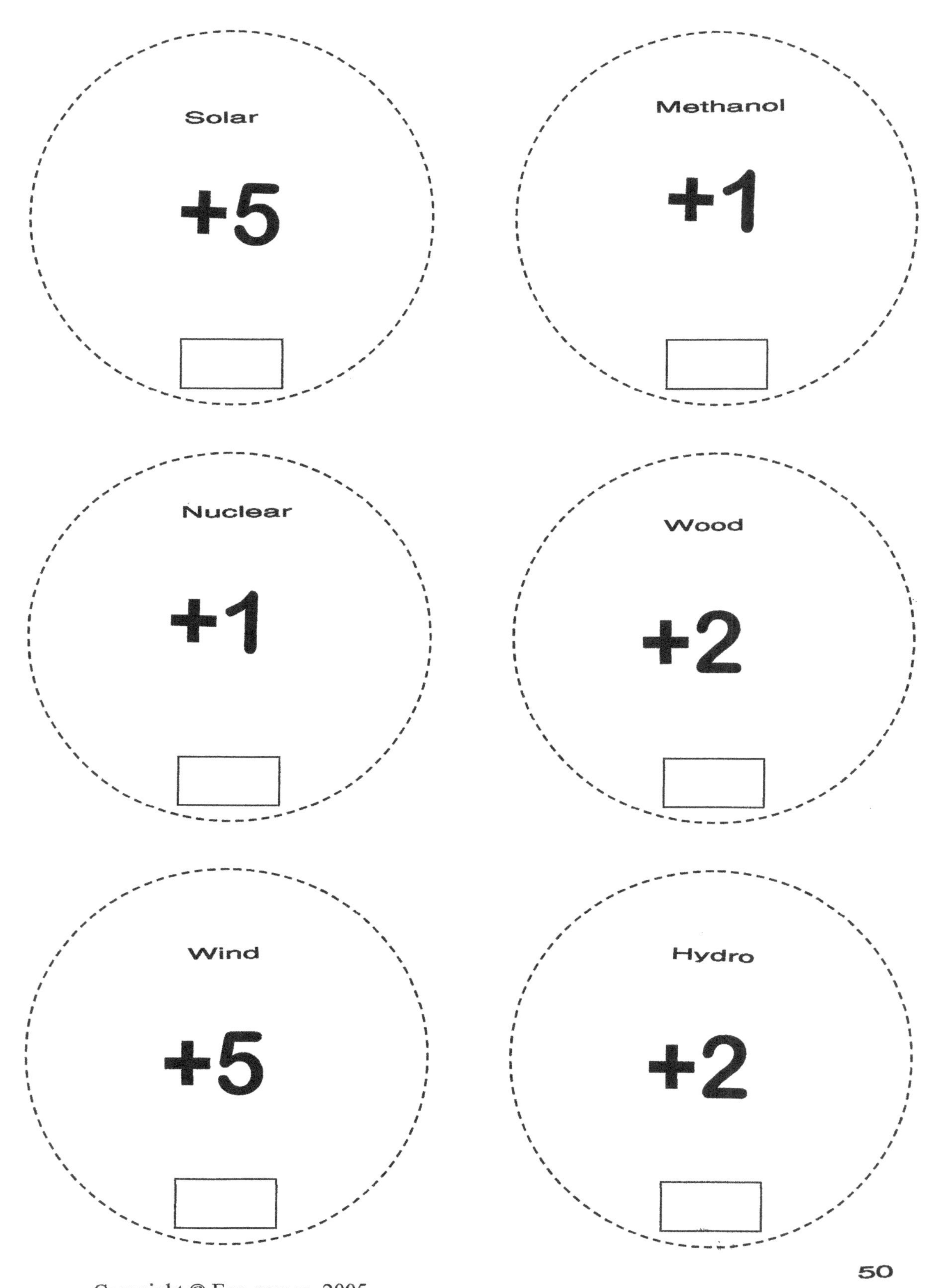

Solar
+5
Methanol
+1
Nuclear
+1
Wood
+2
Wind
+5
Hydro
+2

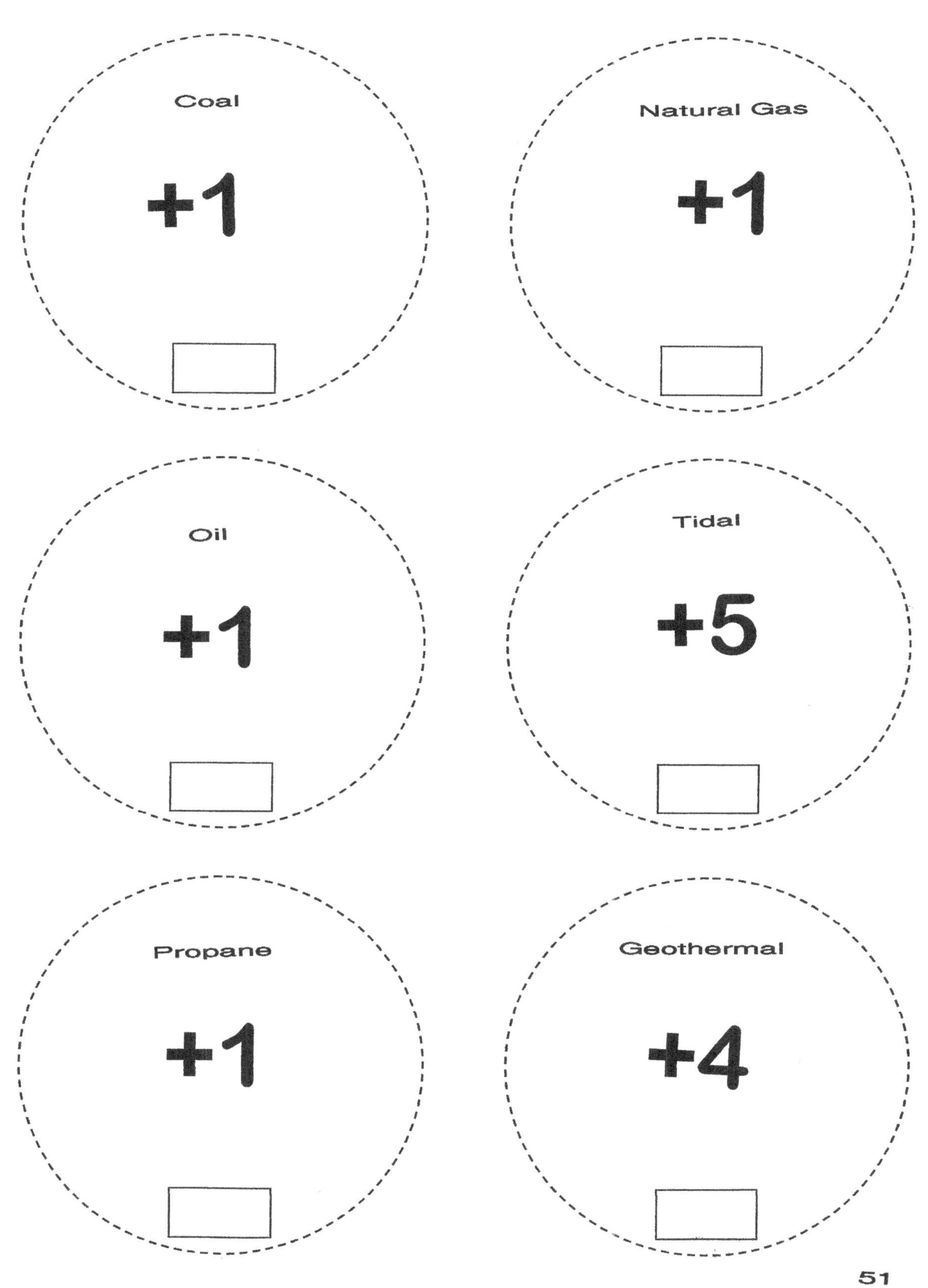

Coal
+1
Natural Gas
+1
Oil
+1
Tidal
+5
Propane
+1
Geothermal
+4

The Energy Game		**Name:**	**Points:**
Solar +5	Methanol +1	Nuclear +1	Wood +2
Coal +1	Global Warming -1	Escaped Heat -1	Natural Gas +1
Wind +5	Acid Rain -1	Power Plant Manager +1/-1	Hydro +2
Oil +1	Tidal +5	Propane +1	Geothermal +4

The Energy Game		**Name:**	**Points:**
Solar +5	Methanol +1	Nuclear +1	Wood +2
Coal +1	Global Warming -1	Escaped Heat -1	Natural Gas +1
Wind +5	Acid Rain -1	Power Plant Manager +1/-1	Hydro +2
Oil +1	Tidal +5	Propane +1	Geothermal +4

The Wetland Ecosystems Game

Ecological Explanation

Wetlands support an incredible diversity of life. Teachers are encouraged to play The Wetlands Game prior to taking a trip to a real wetland (or if it is difficult to visit one) in order to familiarize their students with the macroinvertebrates of the wetland and to set them up for classification and ecosystem activities to follow.

If a wetland is healthy, it will be teeming with insects, molluscs and crustaceans. These macroinvertebrates are fascinating to observe because they are smaller than the larger frogs and turtles of the wetland that the students will be more familiar with; yet they are larger than the microorganisms in the wetland and can be seen with the eye. Macroinvertebrates are also fascinating to study because they vary in their sensitivity to pollution, and thus are excellent as indicator species of the health of the wetland and as species that students may classify.

One tool to measure the health of a wetland is dissolved oxygen. The higher the level of dissolved oxygen in a wetland, the healthier it is considered to be. Testing for dissolved oxygen in the water is a fairly complicated process involving chemicals that may dissuade many teachers from using. However, aquatic macroinvertebrates are classified according to their sensitivity to dissolved oxygen, because the more sensitive ones need higher levels of dissolved oxygen in the water to survive than others. If pollutants enter the wetland, such as phosphates and nitrates, they cause microorganisms and bacteria to grow which use oxygen, thereby decreasing the dissolved oxygen levels. This means that only the macroinvertebrates that are tolerant of low levels of dissolved oxygen will be present in that polluted wetland.

Another tool to measure the health of a wetland is pH. Most aquatic invertebrates need a pH level close to 7. Industrial emissions of sulphur dioxide and nitrous oxide mix with water in the atmosphere to create acid precipitation. When this falls into the wetland it lowers the pH, in some cases to the point where the wetland is no longer able to support many kinds of aquatic life.

Specific Instructions

Follow the instructions under the Game Format section of this book. The object of this game is to save as many invertebrates in the wetland as possible. Students search for the aquatic invertebrate game signs that match those on the game card. When they find the proper match, they must record the Morse Code symbol at the bottom of the sign. Part way through the game, introduce the limiting factors of Low Oxygen and Acid Rain. Give the students the two popsicle sticks, which represent one invertebrate each. The boundary patrollers take on the role of Dipnet If the students go out of bounds, they get caught in the Dipnet. The teacher takes on the role of Invertebrate Biologist. At the end of the game, students' points represent the number of aquatic invertebrates they saved. The limiting factors' popsicle sticks represent how many macroinvertebrates succumbed to the low oxygen and acid rain. Give the students the Morse Code Alphabet. They must decode the symbols on the game card. They will end up with 12 letters they must unscramble. The answer is: SAVE WETLANDS.

Extension Activities and Assessment Suggestions

1)Cut out the macroinvertebrates on the game card and classify them in a chart according to sensitivity to dissolved oxygen, Class One being the most sensitive and Class Four being the most tolerant to low dissolved oxygen. See Web Links below for more.

Class One: stonefly nymph; caddisfly larvae.

Class Two: Dragonfly larvae, whirligig beetle, freshwater shrimp; predacious diving beetle.

Class Three: Backswimmer; Giant water bug; water strider.

Class Four: aquatic worm; mosquito larvae.

2) Classify macroinvertebrates using a tree system according to appearance of a shell, legs, wings, body shape, number of tails.

3) Visit a local wetland. Dipnet. It is important to minimize the impact of this very engaging activity on the wetland. Have students share a dipnet. Specify catching macroinvertebrates and leaving the fish, minnows and other highly visible and sensitive animals alone. Look for safe shorelines with shallow water, and keep students out of the water that is prime animal habitat. Set a time limit for the actual dipnetting, and then focus the students on identifying and classifying their catch. Macroinvertebrates are easiest to see in white plastic wash basins. Return the entire aquatic catch to the wetland.

4) Draw the cross section of a wetland and include all plant, vertebrate and invertebrate life.

5) Demonstrate dissolved oxygen and pH tests.

6) Research one or more macroinvertebrates. Create a visual representation of a food web in the wetland based on the research.

7) Research the disappearance of wetlands and make a case for their conservation.

Literacy Links:

Parker, Steven, Pond & River, Dorling Kindersley Publishing Inc., New York, 2000.

Web Links:

www.streamwatch.org for Extension Activity #1.

www.ec.gc.ca for Acid Rain information.

www.nwf.org/wetlands/

www.audubon.org/campaign/wetland

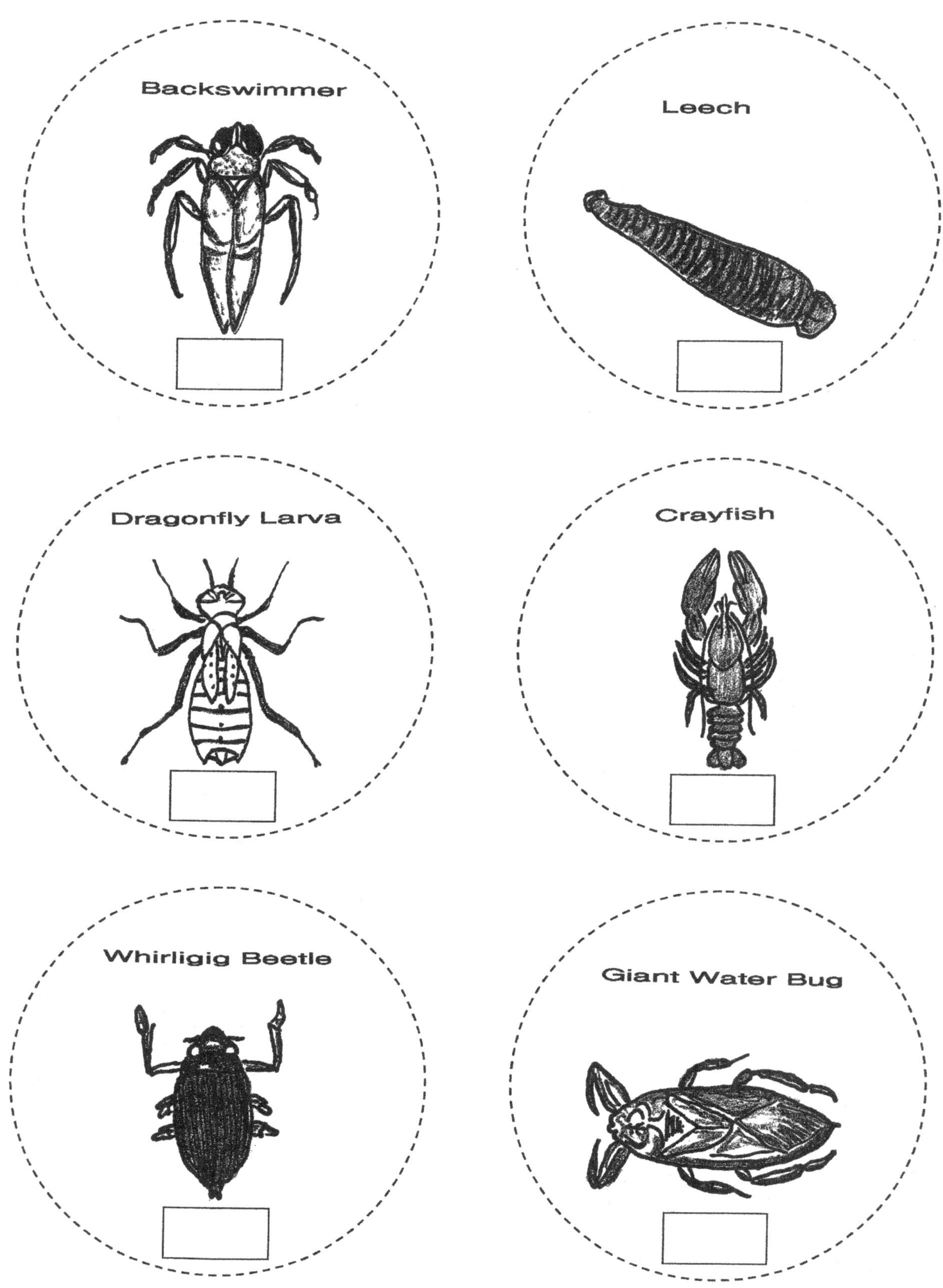
Backswimmer
Leech
Dragonfly Larva
Crayfish
Whirligig Beetle
Giant Water Bug

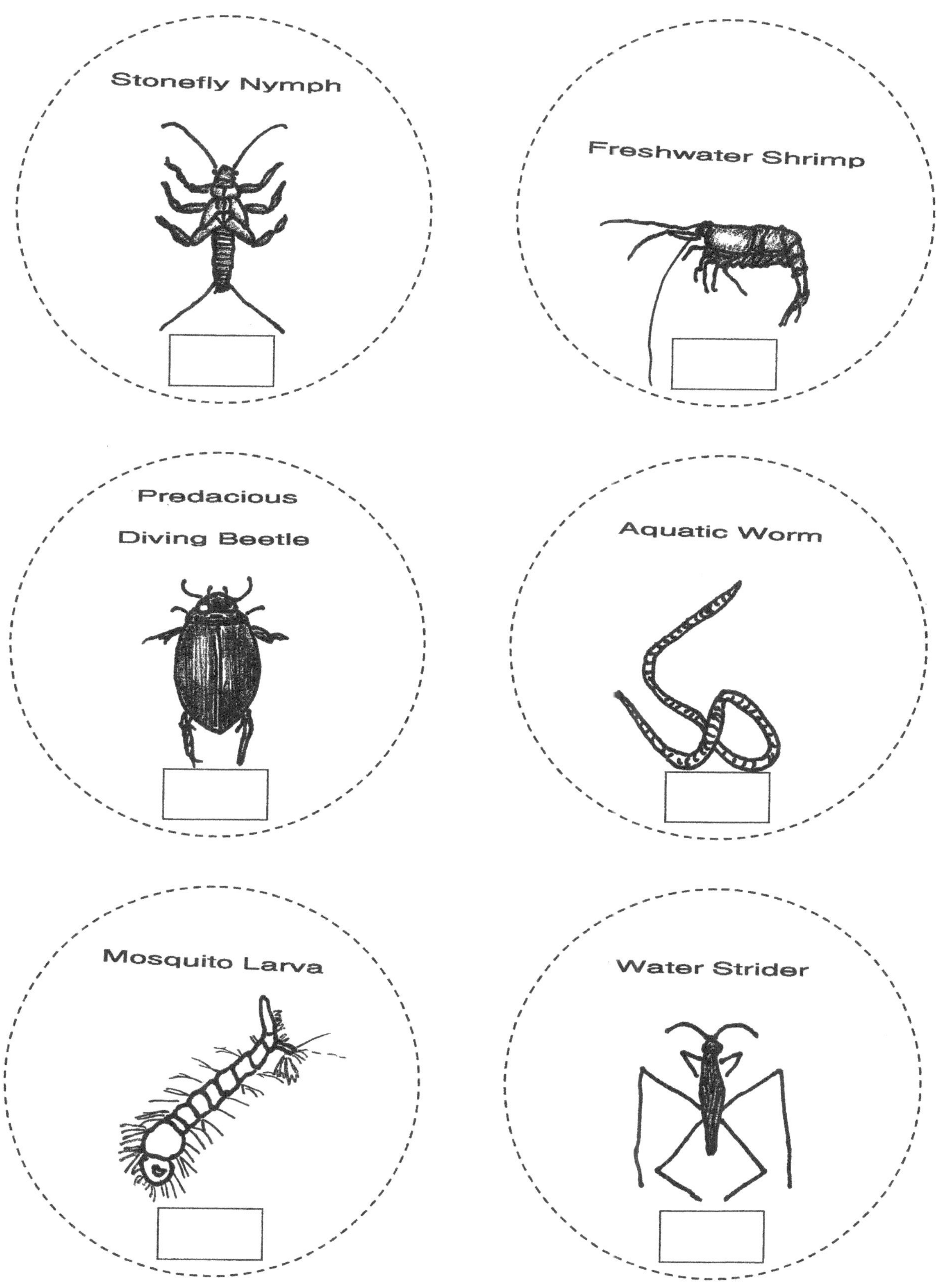
Stonefly Nymph
Freshwater Shrimp
Predacious Diving Beetle
Aquatic Worm
Mosquito Larva
Water Strider

<table>
<tr><td colspan="2">The Wetland Ecosystem Game</td><td>Name:</td><td>Points:</td></tr>
<tr><td>Backswimmer </td><td>Leech </td><td>Dragonfly Larva </td><td>Crayfish </td></tr>
<tr><td>Whirligig Beetle </td><td>Low Oxygen</td><td>Dip-net</td><td>Giant Water Bug </td></tr>
<tr><td>Stonefly Nymph </td><td>Acid Rain</td><td>Invertebrate Biologist</td><td>Freshwater Shrimp </td></tr>
<tr><td>Predacious Diving Beetle </td><td>Aquatic Worm </td><td>Mosquito Larva </td><td>Water Strider </td></tr>
</table>

<table>
<tr><td colspan="2">The Wetland Game</td><td>Name:</td><td>Points:</td></tr>
<tr><td>Backswimmer </td><td>Leech </td><td>Dragonfly Larva </td><td>Crayfish </td></tr>
<tr><td>Whirligig Beetle </td><td>Low Oxygen</td><td>Dip-net</td><td>Giant Water Bug </td></tr>
<tr><td>Stonefly Nymph </td><td>Acid Rain</td><td>Invertebrate Biologist</td><td>Freshwater Shrimp </td></tr>
<tr><td>Predacious Diving Beetle </td><td>Aquatic Worm </td><td>Mosquito Larva </td><td>Water Strider </td></tr>
</table>

<u>**The Carbon Cycle Game**</u>

Ecological Explanation

The element carbon is the main chemical constituent of all organic matter. In other words, all life is based on carbon.

Many students grasp the concept of water moving in a cycle quite easily, as they can observe it first hand in a closed container with a little bit of water in it. The carbon cycle is much more difficult to demonstrate and understand because it occurs on a global scale.

Carbon is stored in major sinks on the planet. Here's the approximate breakdown.

Sink	Amount in Billions of Tons
Atmosphere	578 (as of 1700)–766 (as of 1999)
Soil Organic Matter	1,500-1,600
Ocean	38,000 – 40,000
Marine Sediments and Sedimentary Rocks	66,000,000 to 100,000,000
Terrestrial Plants	540 – 610
Fossil Fuel Deposits	4000

Carbon attaches to two oxygen molecules to make carbon dioxide. Plants absorb carbon dioxide and via photosynthesis convert it to carbon-based sugar molecules. This forms the bases for food for all life on the planet. Dead organic matter over millions of years turns into fossil fuels such as coal and oil.

Carbon dioxide enters the waters of ocean and lakes from the atmosphere via diffusion. Certain forms of sea life such as coral use the form of calcium carbonate to produce their body parts. When they die, they sink to the ocean floor to produce carbonate-rich deposits, such as limestone and dolomite.

Scientists believe the carbon cycle- meaning the absorption and release of carbon from and into the atmosphere- has been in balance for millions of years.

Since the beginning of the industrial revolution, atmospheric concentration of carbon dioxide has increased nearly thirty percent. This is due to the human combustion of fossil fuels. Carbon dioxide is a greenhouse gas. This means that it traps the outgoing energy from solar radiation, which is causing the earth's average temperature to rise.

In the carbon cycle game students are introduced to the major carbon sinks on the planet, and the greenhouse effect from human activity caused by releasing carbon dioxide into the atmosphere via the combustion of fossil fuels. Because climate change is related to carbon dioxide emissions, there are weather symbols on the game signs.

Specific Instructions

In the Carbon Cycle Game, students must run around the playing area and search for twelve game signs, each with a picture and name of a carbon sink. When they find a game sign, they write the Morse code symbol in the box on the game card that matches the game sign. The boundary patrollers take on the role of photosynthesis. The educator troubleshoots in the game as the scientist.

Part way through the game, blow the whistle and have students come back to home base. The educator chooses two students to be the limiting factors of fossil fuel combustion and global warming. The remaining students get two Popsicle sticks, which each represent a single carbon molecule. Begin the game again and follow the instructions in the Game Format chapter.

Blow the whistle at the end of the game to signal all students to return to home base. Tally up the points. The points on a game card represent the number of carbon molecules that player saved. The Limiting Factors' Popsicle sticks represent the number of carbon molecules that succumbed to fossil fuel combustion and global warming..

Give the students the Morse code alphabet. Students must decode the Morse code alphabet into English letters and then unscramble the letters to find the secret environmental message: CONSERVE FUEL.

Extension and Assessment Suggestions
Students could:
1) Draw a diagram of the carbon cycle including major carbon sinks and label arrows indicating the flow of carbon;
2) Investigate ways that they contribute in the burning of fossil fuels and brainstorm ways to conserve fossil fuels;
3) Research and present their findings on local, national and international policies and laws that involve fossil fuel use, combustion and conservation in relation to global warming;
4) Investigate weather symbols.

Web Links
www.physicalgeography.net
www.epa.gov/globalwarming
www.davidsuzuki.org

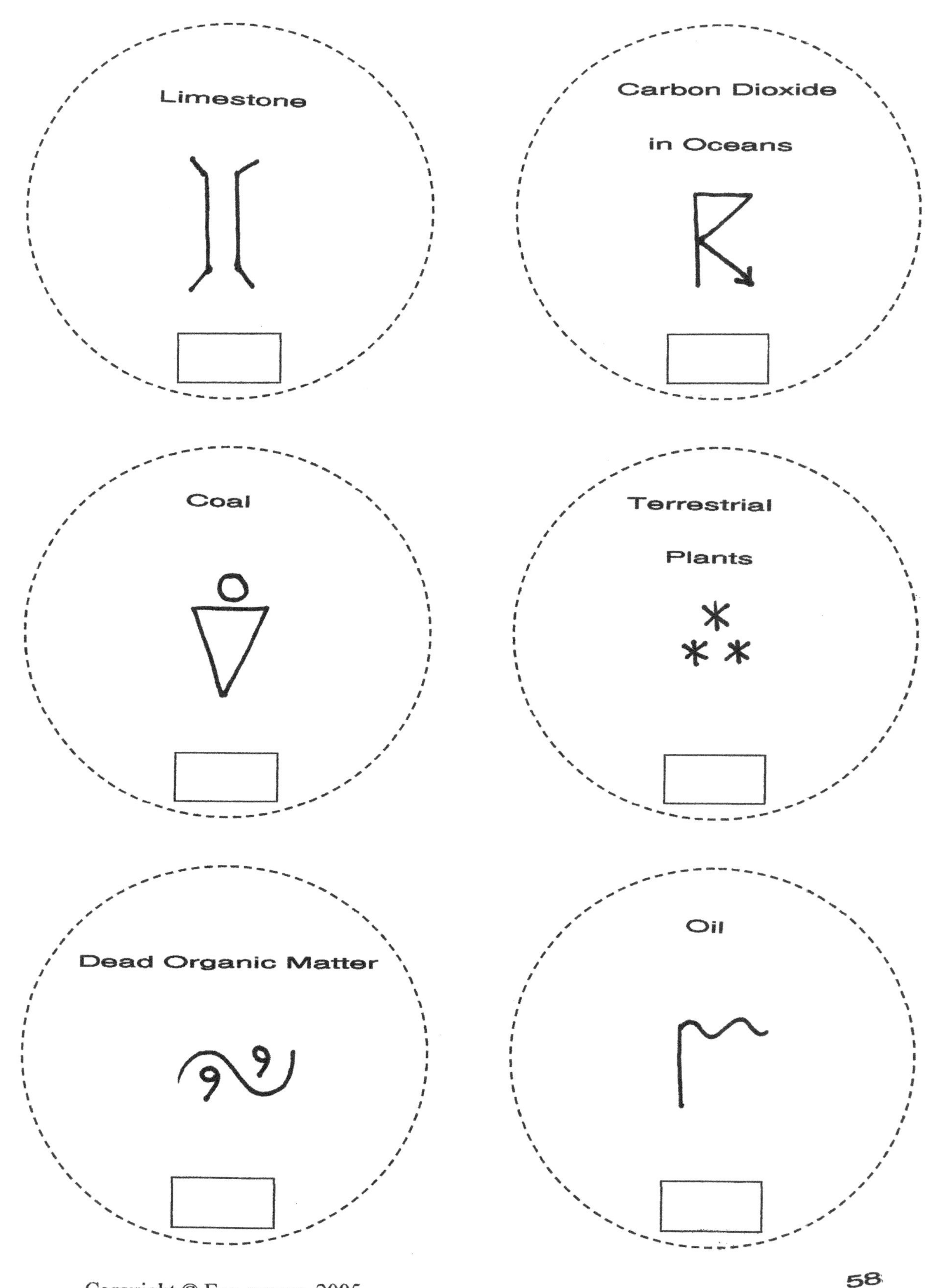

Limestone
Carbon Dioxide
in Oceans
Coal
Terrestrial
Plants
Dead Organic Matter
Oil

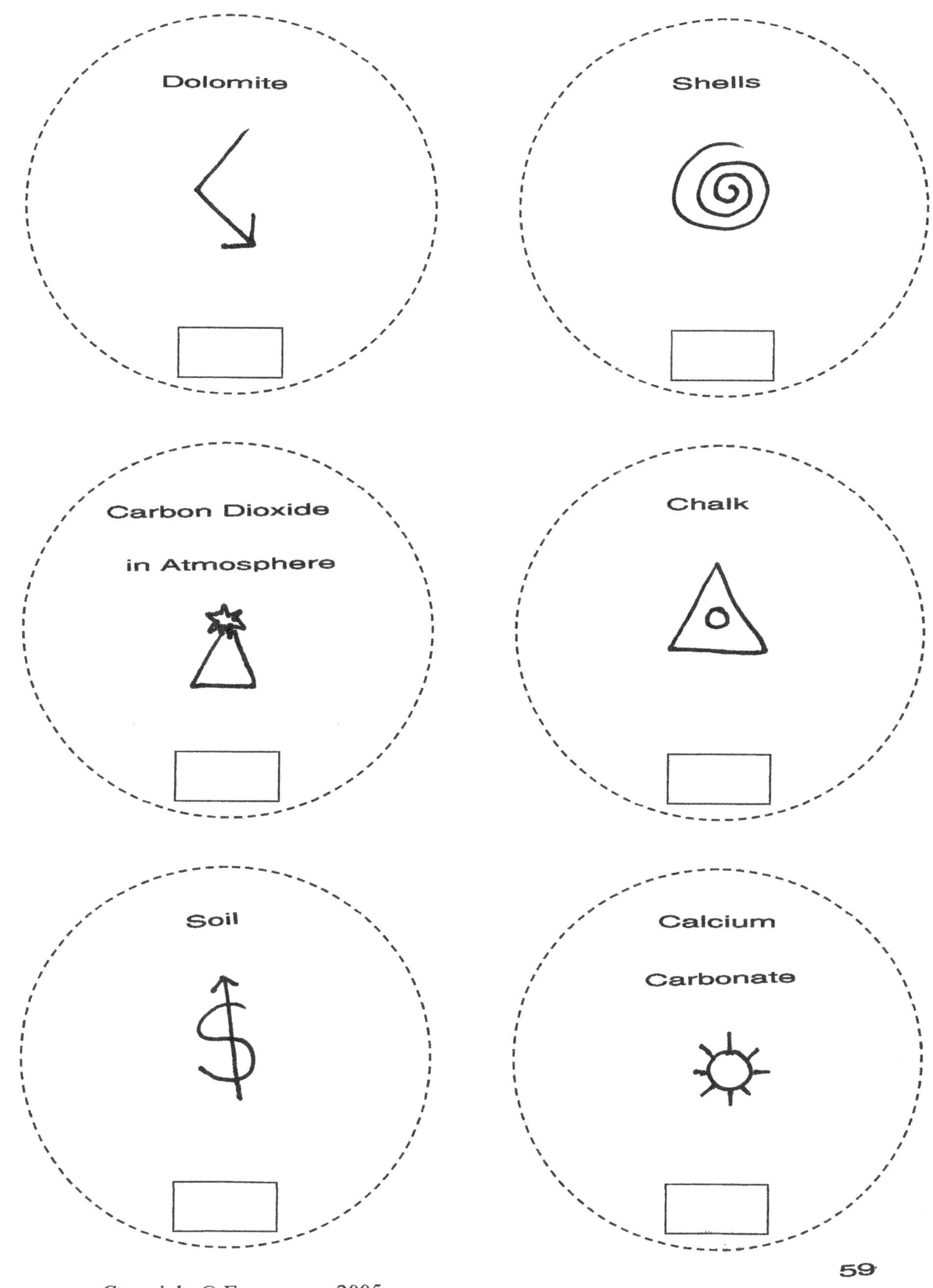

Dolomite
Shells
Carbon Dioxide
in Atmosphere
Chalk
Soil
Calcium
Carbonate

The Carbon Cycle Game		Name:	Points:
Limestone	Carbon Dioxide in Oceans	Coal	Terrestrial Plants
Dead Organic Matter	Fossil Fuel Combustion	Photosynthesis	Oil
Dolomite	Global warming	Climatologist	Shells
Carbon Dioxide in Atmosphere	Chalk	Soil	Calcium Carbonate

The Carbon Cycle Game		Name:	Points:
Limestone	Carbon Dioxide in Oceans	Coal	Terrestrial Plants
Dead Organic Matter	Fossil Fuel Combustion	Photosynthesis	Oil
Dolomite	Global warming	Climatologist	Shells
Carbon Dioxide in Atmosphere	Chalk	Soil	Calcium Carbonate

The Water Systems Game

Ecological Explanation

Over seventy per cent of the Earth's surface is covered with water. Water connects us all. People say "you are what you eat," but more correctly you are what you eat, as the body is similarly over seventy per cent water.

The smallest animals in the world, the microorganisms, live in water, and the largest animals in the world, the whales, live in water. Without water, nothing on the planet could survive.

From outer space, our planet looks like a big blue marble suspended the infinite blackness of outer space. Astronauts remark on its beauty, its fragility and its smallness from the perspective of space. This is a perspective everyone from which all beings on the planet Earth could benefit.

In this game students are introduced to the names of the many systems in which water exists and some of the problems associated with our water systems.

Water systems all over the planet are polluted. Oil spills are one of the major causes of this pollution. Since 1970, about 50 oil spills the size of the Exxon Valdez or larger have occurred internationally. Our water systems are also contaminated with heavy metals, harmful bacteria and other toxins that can harm the living things that live in and ingest the water.

Water systems also do not follow political boundaries. Although over seventy per cent of the world is covered with water, less that one per cent is fresh and clean enough for human consumption. The world's supply of fresh drinking water is not evenly distributed amongst the world's human population. Water diversion projects and dams that bring water to one political state and stop it from flowing to another are the cause of political disruption. As the world population continues to grow and the demand for water grows with it, so will the political upheaval caused by conflicts over the demands for water.

Specific Instructions

In the Water Systems Game, students must run around the playing area and search for twelve game signs, each with a water systems name and symbol. When they find a game sign, they write the Morse code symbol in the box on the game card that matches the game sign. The boundary patrollers take on the dry land. The

educator troubleshoots in the game as the conservation officer.

Part way through the game, blow the whistle and have students come back to home base. The educator chooses two students to be the limiting factors of pollution and built obstruction. The remaining students get two Popsicle sticks, which each represent a single water system. Begin the game again and follow the instructions in the Game Format chapter.

Blow the whistle at the end of the game to signal all students to return to home base. Tally up the points. The points on a game card represent the number of water systems that player saved. The Limiting Factors' Popsicle sticks represent the number of water systems that succumbed to pollution and built obstructions.

Give the students the Morse code alphabet. Students must decode the Morse code alphabet into English letters and then unscramble the letters to find the secret environmental message: CLEAN UP WATER.

Extension and Assessment Activities

Students could:

1) research a major river dam project and all of the effects it has on the plants, animals and local people of the area and present their findings to the class;
2) research and present on a major oil spill in recent history and the effects it has on the environment;
3) conduct a water audit and come up with ways to conserve water at home and school.
4) clean up a local water system;
5) map their local watershed and include all of the aspects of the built environment onto the map, such as water treatment facilities and sewers;
6) research the nautical alphabet symbols used on the game signs and game card.

Literacy Links

Cummings, Barbara J. Dam the rivers, Dam the people. London: Earthscan Publication Inc., 1990

Mitchell, John C. *In the Wake of the Spill: Ten Years after the Exxon Valdez.* National Geographic, Vol.195, No.3, March 1999.

Web Links

www.itopf.com Effects of marine oil spills.
www.pearson.college.uwc.ca The James Bay Hydro-electric project and effects on Cree.
www.greentreks.org Action Projects

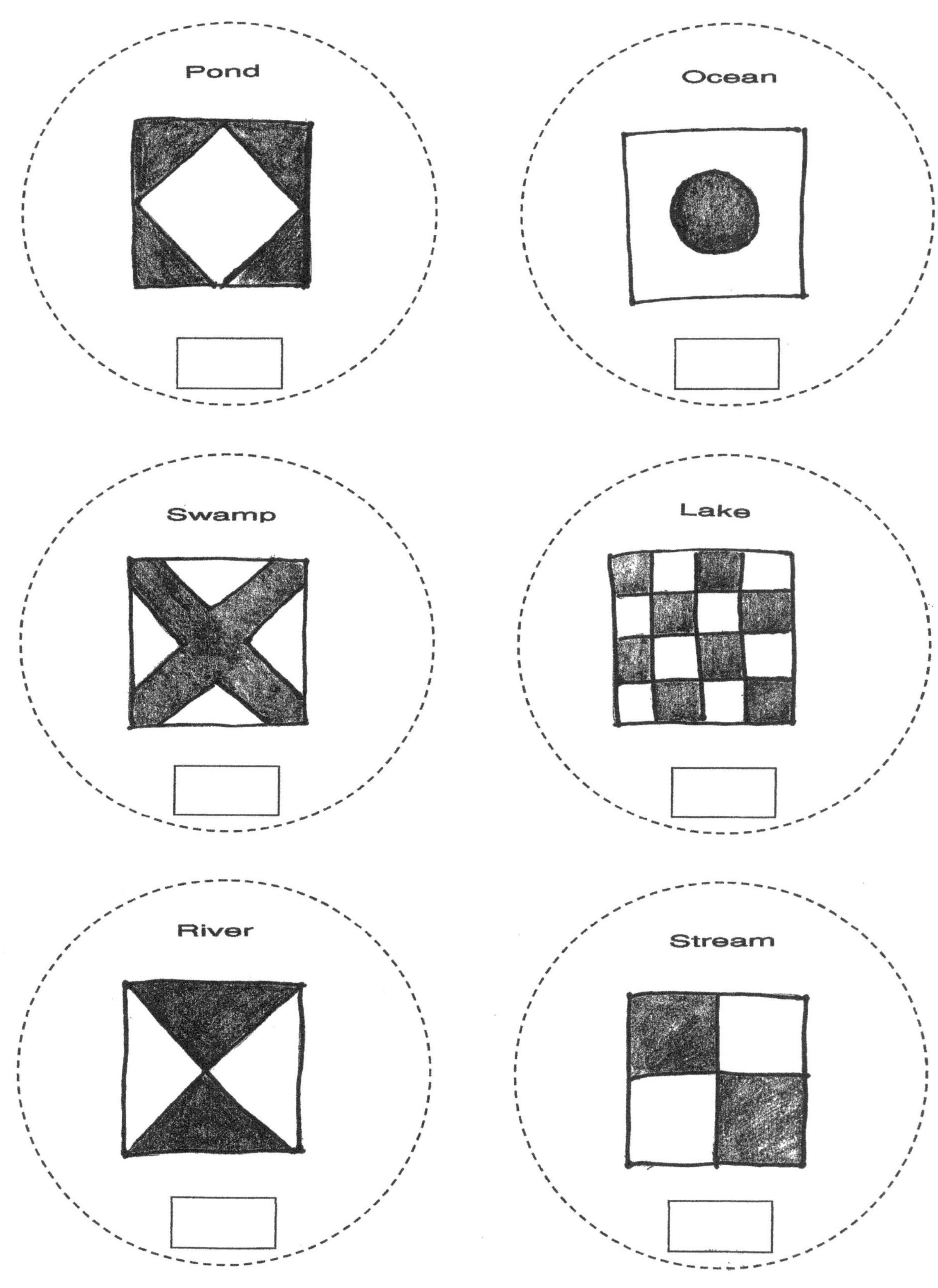
Pond
Ocean
Swamp
Lake
River
Stream

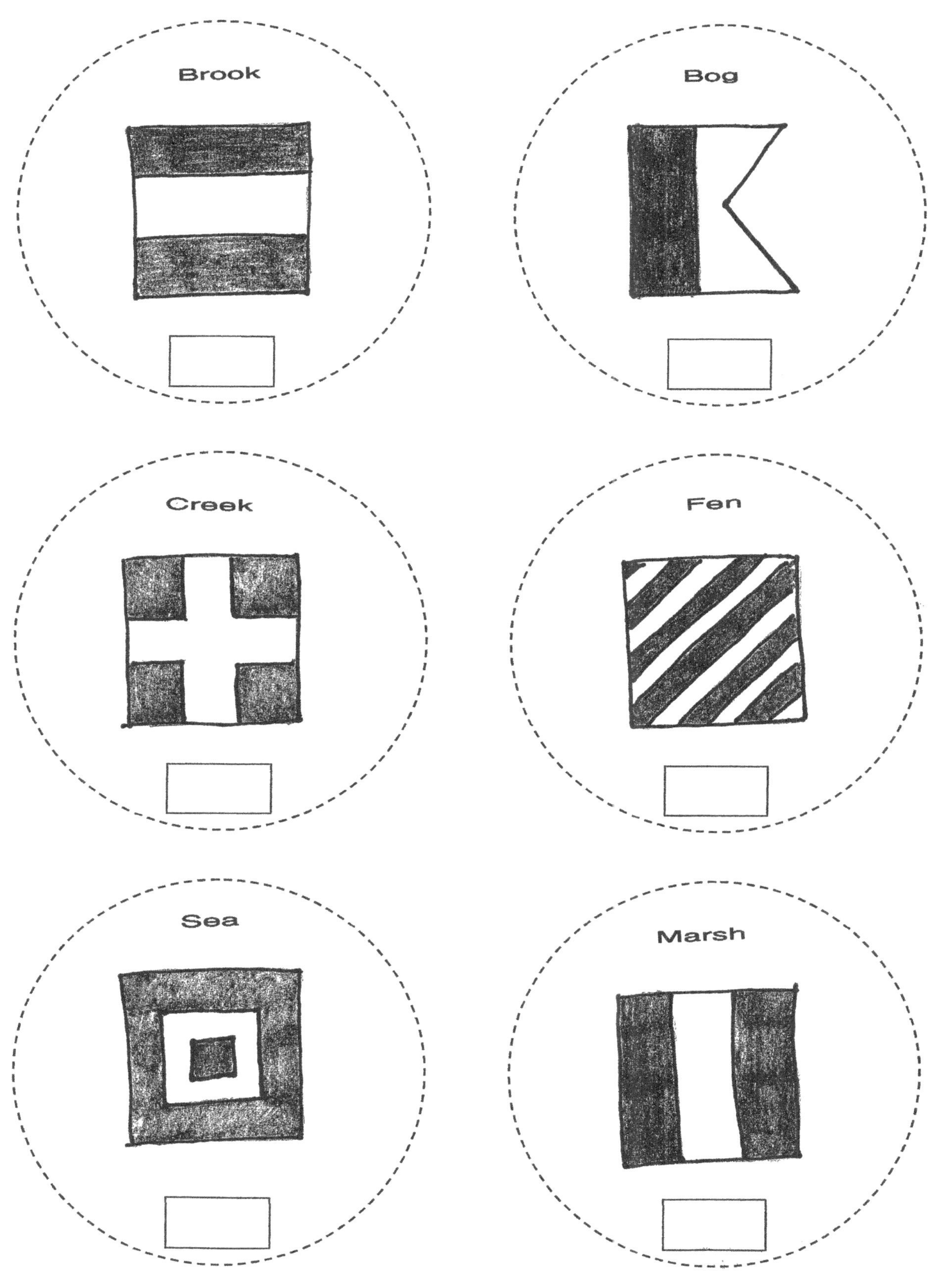

Brook
Bog
Creek
Fen
Sea
Marsh

<table>
<tr><td colspan="2">The Water Systems Game</td><td>Name:</td><td>Points:</td></tr>
<tr><td>Pond</td><td>Ocean</td><td>River</td><td>Stream</td></tr>
<tr><td>Swamp</td><td>Pollution</td><td>Dry Land</td><td>Lake</td></tr>
<tr><td>Brook</td><td>Built Obstruction</td><td>Marine Biologist</td><td>Bog</td></tr>
<tr><td>Creek</td><td>Fen</td><td>Sea</td><td>Marsh</td></tr>
</table>

<table>
<tr><td colspan="2">The Water Systems Game</td><td>Name:</td><td>Points:</td></tr>
<tr><td>Pond</td><td>Ocean</td><td>River</td><td>Stream</td></tr>
<tr><td>Swamp</td><td>Pollution</td><td>Dry Land</td><td>Lake</td></tr>
<tr><td>Brook</td><td>Built Obstruction</td><td>Marine Biologist</td><td>Bog</td></tr>
<tr><td>Creek</td><td>Fen</td><td>Sea</td><td>Marsh</td></tr>
</table>

The Planet Earth Game

Ecological Explanation

Whether one's view is religious, philosophical or scientific, life on earth is a miracle. We are fascinated with the search for life on other planets, but so far that search has proved to be elusive. Again, no matter what one's view, it is becoming increasingly undeniable that all life on our planet in inextricably connected.

Planet Earth contains an incredible diversity of plant and animal life. This life depends on the elements, without which any one life could not exist.

And yet the incredible tragedy exists today that the human animal is altering the natural environment to such an extent that there is a mass extinction of plants and animals. We are altering our climate by burning the finite supply of fossil fuels that took millions of years to form.

We are changing the vital layers of the atmosphere, such as the ozone layer, which allows harmful ultraviolet light from the sun penetrate through the ozone layer and effect plants and animals in ways scientists are just beginning to discover.

Amongst human populations, there is also a tragic pattern of have and have not nations, where the poorest of the poor people on the planet do not have the essential necessities for life and the rich have so much abundance that they are wasteful of material items more than at any other time in human history.

When students begin to understand the massive environmental problems on our planet, they can feel overwhelmed. These great feelings of anxiety come from the deep understanding of knowing one's own connection to the planet, and caring deeply about life on Earth. It is so important for adults to facilitate the emotional energy youth bring to environmental issues into positive action project. Remember: children and youth are the biggest factors in positive environmental change. Children are the future!

The books in the Literacy Links section introduce these problems using a micro-perspective that is much easier for students to identify with.

In the Web links, there are web sites wherein students can challenge themselves to change small habits, that when combined with many other people on the planet, have the potential to huge positive environmental impacts.

The most important concepts for students to walk away with from The Planet Earth Game is that all life on the planet is connected, and that even small changes and positive actions can make a difference.

Specific Instructions

In the Planet Earth Game, students must run around the playing area and search for twelve game signs, each with a name of an essential part of life on Earth and a symbol. When they find a game sign, they write the Morse code symbol in the box on the game card that matches the game sign. The boundary patrollers take on the role of outer-space. The educator troubleshoots in the game as the United Nations official.

Part way through the game, blow the whistle and have students come back to home base. The educator chooses two students to be the limiting factors of global warming and ozone depletion. The remaining students get two Popsicle sticks, which each represent a single species. Begin the game again and follow the instructions in the Game Format chapter.

Blow the whistle at the end of the game to signal all students to return to home base. Tally up the points. The points on a game card represent the number of species that player saved. The Limiting Factors' popsicles represents the number of species that succumbed to global warming and ozone depletion.

Give the students the Morse code alphabet. Students must decode the Morse code alphabet into English letters and then unscramble the letters to find the secret environmental message: LOVE THE EARTH, SAVE OUR WORLD or WE ALL CONNECT.

Extension Activities and Assessment Suggestions:

1) Draw a web of all 12 elements on the game card and label the arrows in order to explain the connections.
2) Research space symbols. The ones in The Planet Earth Game represent the planets, sun, moon and a star. Discover which symbol represents which planet.
3) Research the Nature Challenges from the web sites below and try to follow them.
4) Do a garbage, water or energy audit and come up with doable steps to conserve resources.

Literacy Links

Grant, Tim and Gail Littlejohn. Teaching Global Warming. British Columbia: New Society Publishers.

Miller, Joe. If the Earth were a few feet in diameter. Singapore: The Greenwich Workshop Press, 1998.

Schimmel, Schim. Dear Children of the Earth. Japan, Creative Publishing International, 1994.

"How to Save the Earth." Time Magazine. August, 2002 (On Youth and Environment).

Web Links

www.davidsuzuki.org and link to Nature Challenge.
www.skyfishproject.org
www.greennature.com for information on ozone depletion.

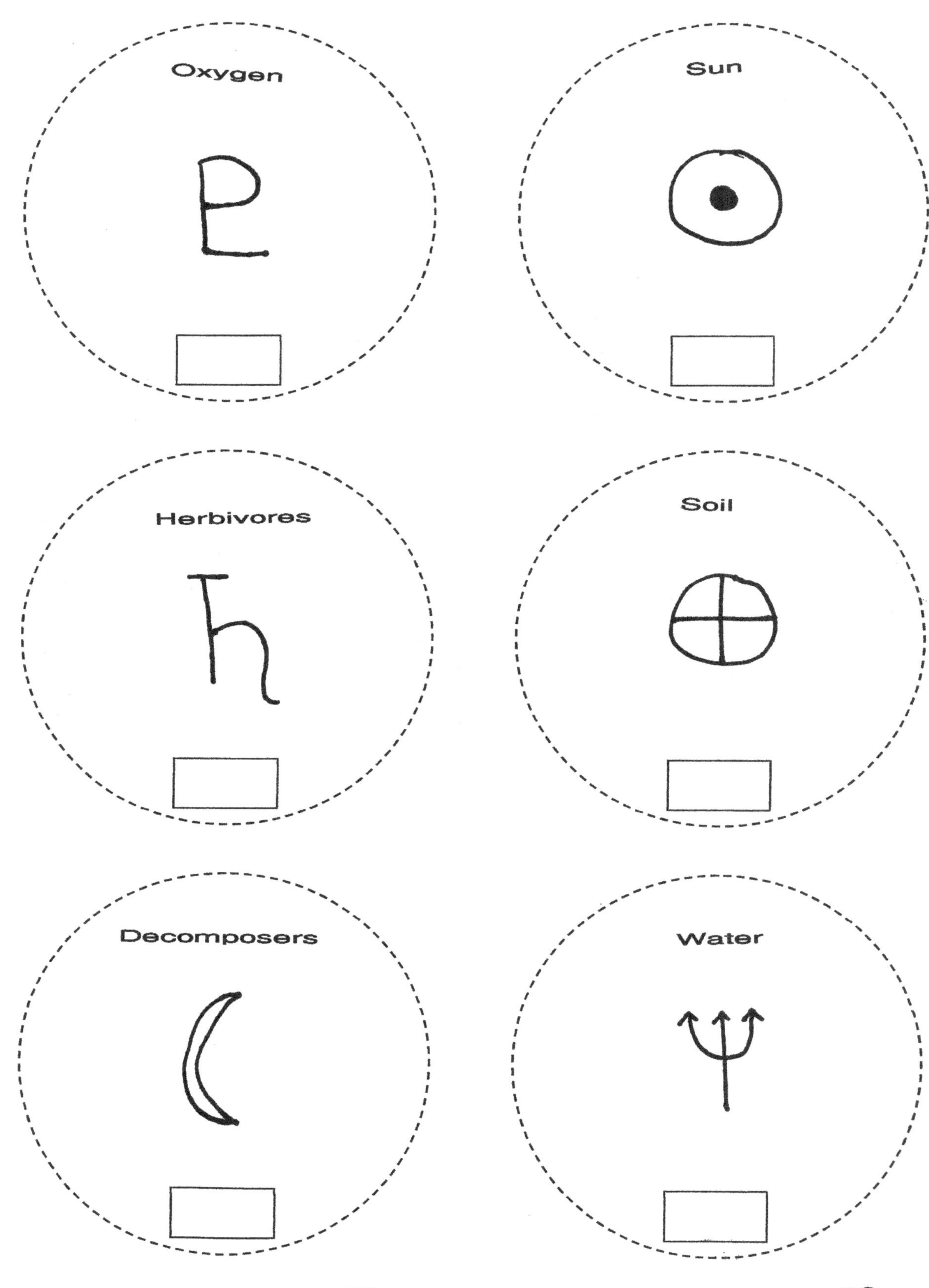

Oxygen
Sun
Herbivores
Soil
Decomposers
Water

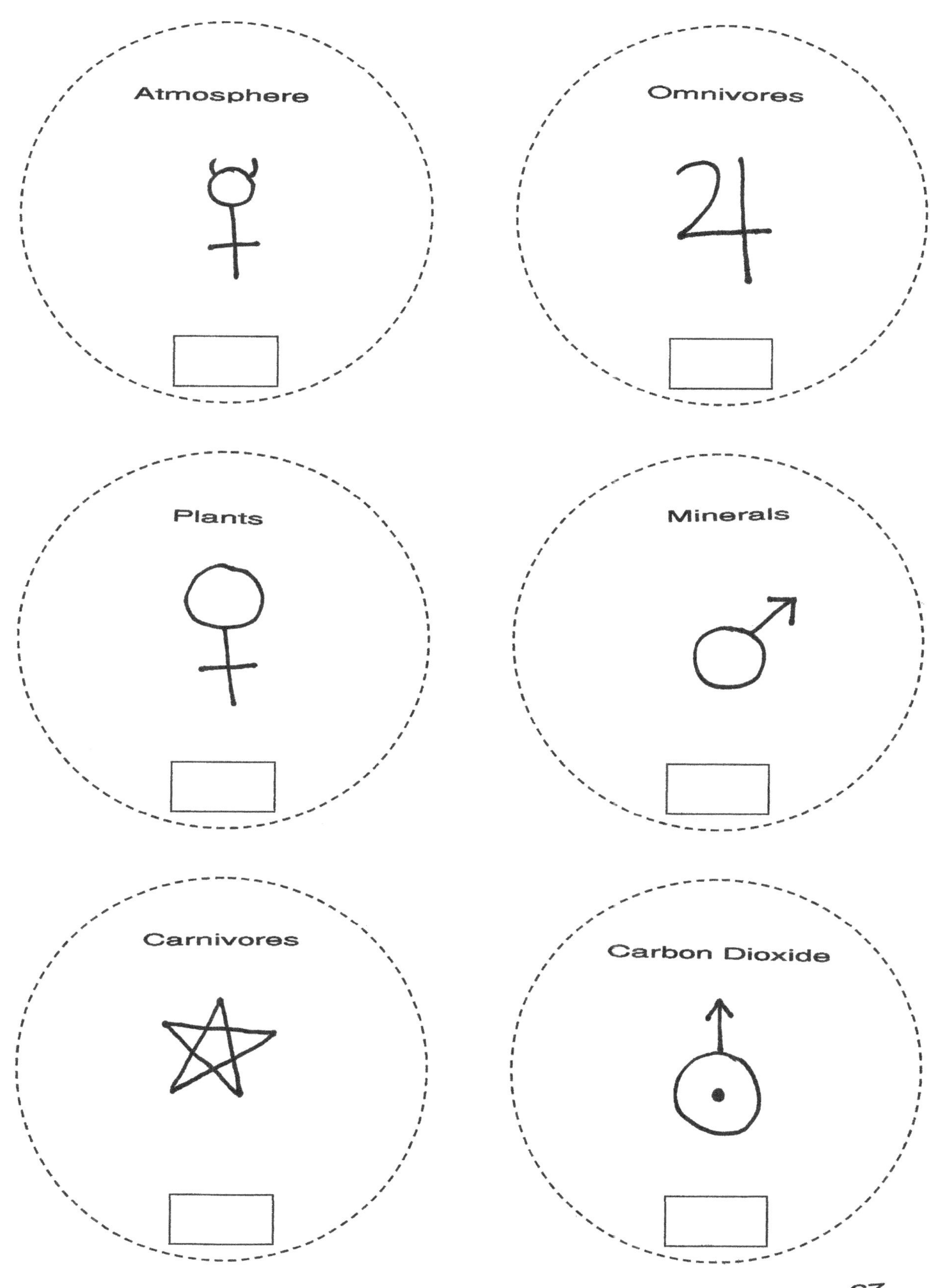

Atmosphere
Omnivores
Plants
Minerals
Carnivores
Carbon Dioxide

The Planet Earth Game		Name:	Points:
Oxygen	Sun	Herbivores	Soil
Decomposers	Global Warming	Outer Space	Water
Atmosphere	Ozone Depletion	World Health Officer	Omnivores
Plants	Minerals	Carnivores	Carbon Dioxide

The Planet Earth Game		Name:	Points:
Oxygen	Sun	Herbivores	Soil
Decomposers	Global Warming	Outer Space	Water
Atmosphere	Ozone Depletion	World Health Officer	Omnivores
Plants	Minerals	Carnivores	Carbon Dioxide

<u>**Applying Mapping and Orienteering Skills**</u>

The instructions for all of the games entail students searching for game twelve game signs at random. Every game can be adapted in the same way in order to have students apply mapping and orienteering skills to the games.

To start, one has to make a map of the schoolyard. This does not have to be as difficult as it sounds at first consideration. What is most likely the case is that a school administrator or caretaker will have the blueprints for the site. Ask to see it and trace a basic outline of the buildings, boundaries, playground and any other features that you will represent on your legend and use in the games. The two best books that I have found for teaching yourself and students about maps and mapping skills are listed below. If blueprints do not exist you will have to make the map from scratch. You could use measuring devices and create an accurate to scale map, or you could simply estimate the size and shape of the building in relation to the boundaries and rough in the other important features. The students will let you know if your map is inaccurate, and you can always revise it.

Remember to orient your map to the north while you are creating it. Draw in a basic compass with the cardinal directions. Add a legend with the most significant features that you have represented on your map. Involve the students with the above process.

Make the map large enough that the whole class can see it when you are explaining how to use it: white Bristol board works well. Laminate it so that you can take it and lay it on any surface in order to explain it to the class outside as well. You could also make smaller maps for the students to hold and use.

Next, decide where you will hide the game signs. Number the game signs. Number the hiding spots on the map so that each numbered hiding spot matches the number on a specific game sign.

In class, go over how to use the map. Explain directions, symbols on the legend, boundaries and home base. Have students work in partners. One student carries the game card. The other student carries the writing utensil.

Outside, meet at home base. Orient the map to the north. Have students physically point to the cardinal directions. Remember them by these sayings for the acronym NESW: Never Eat Shredded Wheat, Never Enter Stinky Washrooms. They tend to go downhill from there.

Assign students two game signs to find. The search is not random. Mark off the two numbers on the game card. Students must use the map to find the game signs. Once they have found the game signs and copied the correct Morse code, they return to you for assessment. You check the card and assign two more game signs. Play all other aspects of the game as per the Game Format instructions and Specific Instructions for each game.

Leedy, Lareen. <u>Mapping Penny's World.</u> New York: Henry Holt and Company, 2000.

Sobel, David. <u>Mapmaking with Children: Sense of Place Education for the Elementary Years.</u> Portsmouth, NH. Heinemann, 1998.

About the Author

Jen has been a teacher specializing in Environmental and Outdoor Education for over thirty years. She hopes to support other educators in connecting students to nature so that they will learn to love it and take care of it. She lives, teaches and plays in Ontario, Canada.

For more information, go to:
www.ecoinquiry.ca